THE OTHER SIDE OF DIPLOMACY

THE OTHER SIDE OF DIPLOMACY

EDITED BY
JAYSHREE MISRA TRIPATHI

Published by Westland Non-Fiction, an imprint of Westland Books, a division of Nasadiya Technologies Private Limited, in 2025

No. 269/2B, First Floor, 'Irai Arul', Vimalraj Street, Nethaji Nagar, Alapakkam Main Road, Maduravoyal, Chennai 600095

Westland, the Westland logo, Westland Non-Fiction and the Westland Non-Fiction logo are the trademarks of Nasadiya Technologies Private Limited, or its affiliates.

ISBN: 9789360459895

10 9 8 7 6 5 4 3 2 1

The views and opinions expressed in this work are the authors' own and the facts are as reported by them, and the publisher is in no way liable for the same.

Typeset by Jojy Philip, New Delhi

Printed at Manipal Technologies Limited, Manipal

Contents

Foreword

The 'other side of diplomacy' is what this book promises the reader, and I, for one, was not disappointed.

Reading the synopsis or the cover, you'd be forgiven for assuming that this is a book that confines itself merely to describing the lived experiences of diplomatic families. However, as you tread through this compendium of fascinating perspectives, you'll soon realise that you're entering a realm that transcends such a simple summary. One of the most captivating things about the stories in this volume is how they are peppered with deeply personal insights, unique to the authors, which make them both more meaningful and readable.

Sharmila Kantha's thoughtfully narrated memories of her husband's first posting in Beijing, where she situates her anecdotes in the broader context of how diplomatic families try to create a sense of belonging in an entirely alien environment.

Given the connotations of elitism and glamour attached to the lives of diplomatic families, this well-compiled anthology provides a nuanced and rejuvenating glimpse into how their experiences are so much more than that. The ordeal of staying away from home, with the spouse working at odd hours, can be quite a daunting experience. Many diplomatic spouses choose to live in their home country and toggle between two (or more!) countries to spend time with their spouse. How do you adapt to daily life in a country that is often entirely unfamiliar—its customs alien, and people diametrically different? What are the deeper layers underpinning the motivational states of the household—a sphere spouses can observe more closely than the diplomats themselves? These are all questions of great value that have rarely been explored with the depth and candour they merit. That unexplored niche is where the current anthology comfortably nestles itself.

It is indeed disappointing that the foreign service still remains a largely male bastion globally. The Women in Diplomacy Index 2022, released by the Anwar Gargash Diplomatic Academy of the UAE, ranked India twenty-sixth in a list of forty countries and the European Union, with only 16.9 per cent of the ambassadorial positions in its missions held by women. The fact that this book features only two male spouses is thus more a reflection of the unfortunate reality of the system than it is of the editor's choices. Perhaps, it is only apt that I write this foreword in the wake of the euphoria surrounding the passage of the Women's Reservation Bill in Parliament, for the contents of this book are sterling illustrations of the qualitative and evaluative significance of women's perspectives on the profession of diplomacy.

Moreover, the spouses included in this anthology are no lightweights in their own professional careers. Hema Devare, who takes us on a beguiling journey to a posting in Sikkim during a transformative moment in postcolonial Indian history, is an illustrious author and public intellectual. So is Kusum Budhwar, whose mantra of 'accept, adapt and assimilate' is perhaps a ringing undertone in the takeaways from a lot of the stories in this collection. Both the diplomatic daughters, Smita Purushottam and Reshmi Ray Dasgupta, are respected minds in their respective fields of foreign service and journalism. Even both the male spouses featured in this anthology, Ashok Pandey and Ajay Shankar, are venerated bureaucrats with tremendous experience in their fields.

Beyond the delicious stories from 'insiders', this book also holds great value for those aspiring for a career in the diplomatic service. Are you ready to be negotiating a historic agreement of the nature of the Indo-Soviet Treaty of Peace, Friendship and Cooperation days after being posted in a country you never expected to be in the first place? Or dealing with a coup in an African country the moment you reach there? From the quotidian details about the day-to-day lives in an international posting to the constant pressures of being on one's toes during contingencies of national interest, this book provides a brilliant glimpse into the kind of lives they can expect to lead, as also the abilities they need to master in order to thrive on the job. Thus situated at diplomacy's intersection with culture and gender studies, this fascinating anthology is sure to enthral all those who want a flavour of the diplomatic life. Even more importantly, by giving a platform to voices that are refreshing, authentic and under-represented in traditional discourse on the subject, it makes a stellar contribution to the democratisation of this discourse.

So, happy reading and bon voyage to the 'other side'!

Dr Shashi Tharoor,
Chairman of the Parliamentary
Standing Committee on External Affairs

Preface

For far too long, the 'voices' of diplomatic spouses have remained unsung. Whilst traversing continents and cultures, supporting our spouses and Missions, raising families in unfamiliar lands, with little or no peer support, we may never forget that there is an unwritten code of conduct—to never embarrass our country or inadvertently cause a diplomatic gaffe or incident.

For many of us who have lived and thrived in difficult or remote postings, in a pre-internet era, there is now a sense of pride and self-assurance that comes from having met or exceeded expectations, having forged connections and representing our wonderful, diverse country overseas. However, there is also a very real sense of having had to put one's own life on pause, even of dismissing one's voice with the official persona. We may be considered 'diplomatic baggage', according to one international best-seller (which I thoroughly enjoyed), but the truth is, there is a lot that goes into this unsung, unofficial role.

At this silver-grey age and life stage, I am privileged and delighted to share several voices with you, through these first-person accounts, to fill in the blanks. Each of us make up a very diverse group and this project has been many years in the making. Over the decades, many of us had often discussed writing about our lives when we got the chance—perhaps after retirement! I decided to ask a few from our service to write their reflections. In this anthology, dear reader, you will embark on journeys from Delhi to Sikkim, to the African continent, through Western, Central, South and Southeast Asia, as well as the Americas and Europe too.

I know this fast-paced, ever-changing world may perhaps not have the inclination to read reflections of older writers, but I cannot let these memories fade into oblivion. There is a need for some calm retrospection, given the disturbing times we live in. Each story does not have to be a protest. Diplomacy, after all, is what happens in the quiet spaces between, not via outrage on social media or sensationalist headlines.

I do hope these 'voices' will resonate and reveal the courage, unwavering determination, resilience and personal growth of diplomatic spouses, who have spent over thirty-five years in service to the nation.

We are very grateful to Westland Books for bringing our 'voices' into print.

Jai Hind!

Jayshree Misra Tripathi

Beyond the Call of Matrimony

RESHMI RAY DASGUPTA

When my mother, Gayatri Ray, joined the band of intrepid women rather tantalisingly called 'External Affairs Wives' in 1953, she was barely twenty-one and had never been abroad—that too on the shoe-string budget that independent India deemed fit for its diplomats (and spouses) to live on in foreign lands. She had to not only adjust to new places, languages and cultures but also to being a spouse, parent, hostess with the mostest, chef and housekeeper, all rolled into one. Back in the day, spouses of Indian diplomats (nearly always wives) had only one choice: make the best of it. Home was far away and lachrymose phone calls complaining about their situation was technologically and financially impossible. Even letters were exchanged fitfully, depending on the vagaries of the ministry's diplomatic bag section, so there was no solace to be found there either. They had to step up to the plate or perish, and they all resoundingly chose the former.

But those were exciting times to live in, especially for my mother, who combined an adventurous spirit with an inquiring mind and a remarkable ability to multitask. Whether it was Karachi or Washington, Dhaka or New York, Berlin or Lagos—and many other postings in between—she took each place as a challenge and an opportunity to understand a foreign land, rather than a duty or a chore. She even got to play a role in the making of history; what more could she want?

Each posting was an adventure and those early diplomats and spouses were pioneers. Often the first to open an Indian mission abroad, the first to spread India's message and pursue her interests, they were like the crew of the Starship Enterprise, going where no Indian had gone before, engaging with new lands and cultures. So, both needed extraordinary abilities not only to acclimatise but also to accommodate. They became true partners in diplomacy.

Today, the internet has made every country familiar; seventy years ago, much of the world was foreign to Indian diplomats and their spouses unless they came from privileged backgrounds. While one partner navigated government and officialdom, the other had to come to grips with a strange country. The language, the lifestyles, the ordinary people, everything was new and needed to be understood. That required not only fortitude but also a sense of humour. Ma would recall how her early struggles with German once led to a peck on the cheek from a shop assistant in Berlin! She had wanted to buy a cushion (kissen in German) and inadvertently said küssen, which means kissing! She soon picked up enough German though to pass through the famous Checkpoint Charlie—then just a barbed-wire gate—into devastated East Berlin and interact with people there over cups of coffee. The despair of a defeated nation was palpable.

Even a mundane task like cooking Indian food was tough abroad. Kitchens were not built for Indian cooking, with turmeric and oil splatters nearly impossible to scrape off tiles and chimneys. Freshwater fish was hard to find, goat meat was available only in Caribbean markets and mustard oil was (and still is, in the US) forbidden as a cooking medium. No one understood the Indian concept of 'jootha' or that vegetarians like Ma would not eat vegetables picked out from a meat dish. Like many spouses, Ma lived and learnt, with personal experience shaping her views.

Travelling by ship to Europe (families were not allowed air travel), she had to go around South Africa, as the Suez Canal was closed due to the second Arab–Israeli war in 1956. She went ashore with friends in Cape Town to shop and post letters. A salesman said he would serve only the lone white woman in their group, who promptly replied she would not care to be served by him, and they all walked out. It was Ma's 'Gandhi-ji at Pietermaritzberg' moment. She resolutely shunned everything South African until apartheid ended thirty-four years later.

She arrived in Washington, DC in the early 1960s—the 'Camelot' years of the Kennedy administration but also the height of the civil rights movement—with a heightened sensibility towards racism. It was a time when 'coloured' people were being assaulted and even killed for entering 'Whites Only' areas. Discrimination was literally brought 'home' to her when they advertised for a house to rent. No offers came from many of the best areas. Then one property owner did call back and, thinking this 'Mrs Ray' was a White American real-estate broker, asked if the diplomat was 'dark' or not. My mother's undiplomatic reply is not difficult to imagine.

They did finally get a house in a nice DC suburb with friendly neighbours. Amid the endless round of mundane chores (Indian salaries at that time did not allow a life of leisure) and diplomatic engagements, Ma followed the progression of the charismatic Dr Martin Luther King, Jr, much like she used to attend morning pravachans by Gandhiji as a teenager in New Delhi. She was inevitably drawn to attend the famous March on Washington and stood among 2,50,000 people to listen to Dr King's powerful 'I Have a Dream' speech in August 1963. Almost exactly three months later, she was in a crowd again, one of the thousands who filed past the closed coffin of the assassinated President John F. Kennedy at the Capitol Building.

Early on in my parents' posting in DC, Prime Minister Jawaharlal Nehru arrived on his third visit to the US. It was a magical time, with banquets, concerts and even a trip to Disneyland and Hollywood, where my mother's dinner partner, Marlon Brando, scribbled Shakespearean sonnets on her napkin. At a White House gala for the visiting Indian leader, she was admiring the paintings when she was tapped on the shoulder. She turned around, and a man said, 'Hello, my name is John. What's yours?' An extraordinary conversation then ensued between a president and a lady. 'Gayatri Ray,' said Ma, awestruck.

'Ray? You're Bengali!' said Kennedy.

She was astounded. 'How did you know I'm Bengali?'

He flashed that famous smile. 'Ray ... like Satyajit Ray, right? So you're Bengali!'

She was floored. Earlier that year (February 1961), Kennedy had watched Ray's *Apur Sansar*, but linking the director's surname to an Indian lady at a party stands testament to his political nous. They chatted for five more minutes, and Ma came away in a fan-girl daze.

Imagine what she felt on 22 November 1963 when she turned on her favourite afternoon soap to hear Walter Cronkite say, 'President Kennedy died at 1 p.m. ... some thirty-eight minutes ago.'

Tears welling in her eyes, she rushed out and, on seeing her neighbour, cried out, 'Mrs Brown, President Kennedy is dead!'

'So what? He's a Democrat,' was the lady's stony-faced reply.

Two days later, Ma stood in the rain to file past his body along with thousands of other ordinary mourners; as a spouse, she did not have access to the officials' queue.

In a way, this sums up the life of an Indian Foreign Service spouse—ordinary and extraordinary at the same time.

Even now, but more so back then, there was an impression that Indian Foreign Service families led charmed lives full of champagne and ballroom dancing. But the truth is, getting on with life in constantly changing circumstances is no party, especially in foreign lands. Its compensation, though, is a chance to participate in making history, even if unacknowledged.

On their first posting to Karachi back in 1953, for example, Ma found herself a confidante of Begum Hamida, the feisty first wife of the then Prime Minister of Pakistan, Mohammad Ali Bogra, thanks to their common roots in East Bengal. Even as a mere Third Secretary's wife, Ma gained unprecedented access to the Pakistan PM's residence because of ... mishti. Living in Karachi, Begum Hamida longed for the familiar sweet taste of Bengal and asked Ma if she would make mishti for her occasionally. How could Ma say no? So, every few weeks Ma would make sandesh, pithey or chomchom and take it to the PM's residence and the two ladies would chat—in Bangla—about everything from food to women's rights. Ironically, the language that bound them eventually led to the split of Pakistan.

Ma recounted how Begum Hamida bristled when a delegation of women arrived at her home to protest about her wearing only saris. They averred that Pakistani women should wear only salwar kameez. Begum Hamida told the protesters forthrightly that being Pakistani had nothing to do with attire, and that she had worn saris since she was fourteen years old and was not about to change now. If only those who caused Pakistan's east–west schism had listened to her.

Just about a decade later, the impact of Pakistan's shortsighted policy towards its Bengali half began to be felt, and my parents were in the thick of it. Posted in Dhaka when the second India–Pakistan war broke out in 1965, Ma was put under house arrest with my ten-year-old brother. My father, then Deputy High Commissioner, was away in New Delhi on consultations, and I was about to be born. So, my nine-months-pregnant mother was alone with her little son, without money or means of communication, and allowed access only to Pakistani doctors.

But she had no time to panic. Indeed, the first thing she did was to calmly burn the cipher books lying in the safe at home. Had my father been there, it would have been his first task. Ma realised India's code books had to be kept away from enemy hands and destroyed them before the Pakistanis came to get them. To this day, I marvel at her presence of mind. As Prime Minister Lal Bahadur Shastri died unexpectedly in Tashkent, she never received the Padma Shri that he had promised her for that act of quick thinking. But doing things beyond the call of duty was just so characteristic of her. Since pregnant women of other nationalities had been airlifted out, Ma could have crumbled and begged to be allowed to go to Singapore as well. However, because she had been singled out for this 'special' arrest, as she was Indian and 'the enemy', Ma decided to fight back. She refused to see any doctor at all and told her Pakistani incarcerators that if she died or lost the baby during childbirth, they would have an international incident on their hands.

The Pakistanis were stumped by her peaceful Gandhian non-cooperation. After some hasty confabulations, they capitulated. They said she would be evacuated, albeit in a military plane with no seats. Ma agreed but demanded to see an American doctor before leaving. They accepted that too. One doughty Indian woman had the Pakistanis beating a retreat in Dhaka!

She only revealed her inner turmoil to Dr Gray, the American obstetrician at Dhaka's Holy Family Hospital, who also happened to be a nun who went by the name Sister Luke.

'I have no money and don't know anyone in Singapore,' said Ma. 'What should I do?'

'Don't worry, the Singapore branch of our hospital will take care of everything, including expenses and contacting your husband,' reassured Dr Gray.

'But what if labour pains start during the flight, as this is the ninth month?' enquired Ma.

'That won't happen,' replied Dr Gray. 'Just pray hard. God will listen.'

Armed with only that double assurance from a doctor–nun, Ma came home and informed the Pakistani military commander that she was ready to leave. He told her to pack a suitcase and wait for a call.

A few days later, the Pakistani military transport plane arrived but had to dump fuel to land on the shorter runway of a secondary airfield, as India had bombed the main airport. Refuelling took time. When the plane was finally ready to fly the next morning, the call came.

Ma said she wanted to listen to radio news before leaving for the airport and tuned in to *Voice of America* and heard that a ceasefire had been declared at 3.30 a.m. that very morning; it was 23 September 1965. She promptly sat down and flatly refused to go.

'The war is over and you can't force me to fly out,' she told the escort party quietly. 'I want to be taken to Holy Family Hospital.'

The Pakistanis were flummoxed again. They had probably never come across such a calmly resolute woman. They went into a huddle. Taking her away forcibly would be dangerous given her condition, but what about that plane, fully refuelled and waiting just for her? They eventually decided not to risk it and the plane returned to West Pakistan. But the Pakistanis had their revenge. They saw to it that my mother and brother's house arrest did not end until my father managed to return to Dhaka three weeks later via Singapore on 16 October. I was born on 18 October at Holy Family Hospital. Someone up there—perhaps my birthplace's guardian goddess Dhakeshwari—had listened to Ma's prayers.

Just six years later, my parents' ties to the land that had been strengthened by my birth was to result in another joint effort during the decisive 1971 Liberation War. Indeed, my parents' involvement in the creation of Bangladesh was straight out of a movie—or, more apt for our times, a web series!

A Muslim League activist at the time, Sheikh Mujibur Rahman, had known my father since their Calcutta University days in the 1940s. As students, they were political and debating rivals, but when they met again at a diplomatic party in Dhaka in 1966, they bonded as two Bangals—East Bengalis. And that instant reconnect triggered a crucial request.

By then, Bengali Pakistanis were already chafing at being constantly belittled, second-guessed and sidelined by their Punjabi- and Urdu-speaking compatriots. At the same time, the Awami League was gaining strength in the more populous eastern province. Sheikh Mujib indicated to my father that he would have to pitch for independence soon. Would India help, was his discreet query. As a fellow Bangal, my father understood his sentiment perfectly, but as an Indian diplomat he needed an official go-ahead to give Sheikh Mujib the answer he sought.

So he headed straight to New Delhi to convey this critical request in person to India's Foreign Secretary, and the two then took the matter to Prime Minister Indira Gandhi, who instantly agreed. My father returned and conveyed the message to Sheikh Mujib.

Thus, a plan was set in motion that led to the creation of Bangladesh five years later. In addition to the military and official diplomatic manoeuvres, this involved numerous backstage operations: to build opinion and create the right optics for the impending break. Ma contributed to this, again beyond the call of duty.

After returning to New Delhi from Dhaka, my parents became friendly with the few Bengalis in the Pakistan mission, including a wonderful, cultured couple with two young daughters with whom we are still in touch. Gradually, the East Pakistani diplomats were motivated to stop putting up with systematic humiliation—such as being assigned only insignificant official work despite seniority—and to defect. Ma played a major role in this persuasion, especially allaying fears about the children's safety.

The day in April 1971 when the Pakistan High Commission was holding an Urdu mushaira became D(efection)-Day, as the Bengali speakers in the mission had little to do for the event. Amid the hubbub, they slipped out unnoticed and made their way to a rendezvous spot in south Delhi. As women were not likely to be tracked by Pakistani intelligence sources, it was decided that Ma would drive them to the 'safe house' in Gurgaon (which was still a village then), where a battery of foreign journalists awaited their arrival. There, the defectors declared their allegiance to a yet-to-be-born Bangladesh and shouted 'Joy Bangla!' for the first time. It was a deeply emotional moment for Ma as well.

My parents' efforts did not end there. My father played a pivotal official role in the 1971 operations, for which he was awarded the Bangladesh Liberation War Honour by Sheikh Hasina, who was then the Prime Minister of Bangladesh, nine years after he had passed away. When Ma went to Dhaka in 2013 to accept that award for my father, one of the diplomats she had driven to Gurgaon in 1971—by then retired and serving as a key advisor to the current PM—confided that he had recommended her for the same honour.

Like the promised Padma Shri, Ma did not get the Bangladesh award either. But that has been the lot of so many diplomatic spouses. Their roles often fall into a grey area, where their contributions are regarded as supplementary or complementary. They may exercise agency and accomplish extraordinary things out of personal conviction and motivation. However, since these efforts do not fall within any official ambit, they are overlooked and sometimes even diminished. Yet, they soldier on.

I remain in awe of the spirit and dedication of foreign service spouses, beyond the call of matrimony.

The Lost Kingdom
Sikkim

HEMA DEVARE

The Indian Foreign Service is indeed a roller-coaster ride. Even before you are ready to depart, you have already landed at the next destination, which is unknown, unfamiliar and uncharted. But it could never be as unique as the one our ride landed us in during the early years of the service. Well settled in the land of milk and honey, the idea of moving from Washington, DC, the coveted capital of the world, seemed very distant. Before we finished our three-year term, during his official visit India's Foreign Secretary spotted my husband—a familiar figure to him from his earlier posting in Moscow—and promptly said, 'You know Sanskrit and Hindi well. So, you are the right candidate to go to Sikkim.'

'Sikkim? Where on Earth is this place?' I thought to myself when we first heard the news. In 1970, Sikkim was like a dot hidden somewhere in the Himalayas, having no status, either as a country or a full state. Why were we being packed off to such a godforsaken place? After living in America, which was everyone's dreamland, penance was expected, but banishment to the Himalayas seemed too severe.

Situated at 5,000 feet, with a population of around fifteen thousand people, Gangtok, the capital of Sikkim, was a so-called foreign posting for an Indian diplomat. But there was no embassy and no other missions. Although an independent kingdom, Sikkim was an Indian protectorate. There was the Maharaja, the Chogyal, on one side, and the Political Officer with the rank of Ambassador, representing the Government of India, on the other. Then there was the large presence of the Indian Army, the 17 Mountain Division responsible for the defence of Sikkim, which was located between India and China.

We looked at the map and read about the living conditions provided by the Ministry of External Affairs, which disclosed that the place was primitive, without basic amenities and infested with leeches.

Of course, the description did not deter the officer in Sudhir, charged with patriotism, ready to face any challenges and excited by the idea of defending the border of India. I, on the other hand, was filled with apprehensions and question marks.

We undertook the journey to Sikkim, first by Assam Mail from Delhi to Siliguri, a thirty-six–hour journey and then began the adventurous and arduous travel to Gangtok. The only mode of transport was a Jeep, which could negotiate mountainous, winding, narrow and dangerous roads. Mountains loomed large on one side and a small road carved through them; a deep valley on the other side had the Teesta River gushing through it. The rocks appeared to be sitting loosely on the hills and could tumble down anytime. Landslides were very common, and if we saw the boulders coming down in the distance, we had to wait for several hours until it stopped.

Nature was imposing and overwhelming, and you always felt like a speck in this universe. This feeling never left you in Sikkim.

When we reached Gangtok after a nearly eight-hour harrowing drive, we were ready to accept whatever fate had in store for us. We thanked the driver constantly for the safe ride.

The sleepy little town of Gangtok became our home. The enormous American car that we had brought somehow miraculously arrived through a long, circuitous route. It was clearly not suited for mountainous roads and soon became a white elephant sitting in the garage. Our house was a cottage in a hill station, built in colonial style, with a front glass veranda offering a magnificent view of the Kanchenjunga range of the Himalayas. The house was on a hillock with a deep forest behind. At night, we saw twinkling glow worms and heard jackals from time to time. Our garden was a great delight. Beautiful sweet peas, gladioli, carnations, nasturtiums and, most of all, orchids that were native to Sikkim adorned the garden. However, one had to be mindful of the leeches. They could only be removed by rubbing salt on the body. When I saw the kitchen, my heart sank. Cooking had to be done on coal fire. I had thought the foreign service was ahead of its time. But here, one was literally going back a century in time.

Life there was like living in a princely state with a real king, queen and princes. The Chogyal, of Tibetan-Bhutia lineage, lived on a hill in a palace that had elegant Tibetan architecture. His family wore Tibetan silk and jewellery, and all Bhutias wore bakus, their native dress. In front of the palace was a small Buddhist chapel where lama dances were held to appease the mountain spirits once a year.

The prevailing religion was Buddhism of the Mahayana sect. After the Dalai Lama moved to India in 1959, other prominent

Buddhist religious leaders also came to India. Gyalwa Karmapa was one of them. He settled down at Rumtek Monastery near Gangtok. The Chogyal regarded him as a religious head. The Tibetan monks from the monastery would often visit Gangtok for their rituals. Hence, lamas were omnipresent in Sikkim.

Whether it was their constant presence, their proximity to the mountains or the overwhelming nature surrounding us, one couldn't shake this constant feeling that life was controlled by supernatural power and was not in your own hands. The people of Sikkim are superstitious and believe in many rituals. We experienced this firsthand when the lamas were called to India House to appease the rain gods so that it would not rain during the Republic Day reception. Call it a coincidence, but in spite of an extremely cloudy sky, it did not rain until the reception was completed. Even in death, the Sikkimese Buddhists wait for the right time for cremation; until then, the body is kept in a seated Buddha position. The monks offer prayers for days on end. Feasts are organised for the lamas and visiting relatives until the cremation is over, which could be a month later. We witnessed this ritual while visiting a friend who was one of the Chogyal's officials, upon his father's death. The Chogyal's family, the Tibetan Bhutias and the palace officials believed in Buddhist rituals and followed them diligently.

The Sikkimese community consisted of Bhutias, Lepchas and Nepalese. Lepchas were the original natives, belonging to the working class, whereas the Bhutias came from Tibet and were the rulers of Sikkim. Bhutias comprised only 15 per cent of Sikkim's population, while 75 per cent were Nepalis who had settled in Sikkim. So, the lingua franca was Nepali. Tibetan and Nepali culture thrived simultaneously in Sikkim. Both communities enjoyed drinking, dancing and merrymaking. They loved to play mahjong and flush. When guests came to Bhutia homes, they were offered chaang, a brew made of barley, and the guest was supposed to drink it with a bamboo straw until the glass was empty and made a slurping sound. All along, the hostess would keep nudging the guest lightly with needles, such was the custom. Thukpa and grilled meat and chicken were their favourite foods. Nepalis celebrated the festivals of Deepavali and Dussehra with decorations and sweets. They would adorn their homes with marigold flowers. They also loved to sing, dance and gamble, with rakshi being their drink of choice.

India House was the Political Officer's residence, which was situated on a hill, and 500 feet below, also on a hill, was the Political Office. India House was a splendid cottage that was the residence of British officers in the nineteenth century. It had the most captivating view of the Kanchenjunga, the highest peak in the mountain range. On a clear day, the peaks would be visible, spread out widely on a cinemascope scale. On cloudy days, they would be completely elusive. India House had a riot of colourful flowers of all varieties.

The Political Officer, First Secretary, Second Secretary and small staff were like a big family. It was extremely important to keep up the morale of the staff since there was no means of entertainment. People often suffered from amebiasis due to the hard mountain water. The army doctor assigned to the Political Office was forever busy attending to patients. The role of the Political Officer's wife became important in this context. She had to look after the staff, their well-being, the condition of their habitat, etc. She started a school for the children of the lower staff, and we all taught there. They were good at music, so there was a lot of singing. We had to organise cultural programmes and children's shows to keep the staff engaged. The children of the Political Office climbed up the hill to attend the English-medium school, Tashi Namgyal Academy, run by the Chogyal.

Our six-year-old daughter attended this school and spoke excellent Nepali, just like the locals, often bursting into Nepalese poetry. Her playmates were Nepalese children from the neighbourhood. With the birth of our second daughter, Aparna, the Himalayas became an inseparable part of our lives, emotionally binding us to this Shangri-La. Everyone was kept busy at the Political Office, with some even displaying quirky behaviour. One officer, in his enthusiasm, used to ride on horseback from his house, which was next to the valley, to India House. He had kept one room in his house especially for his horse and would feed him jalebis. One Private Secretary would often burst into song and recite shayari while working. His officer had to restrain him without losing his cool. On the whole, the atmosphere was friendly and jovial.

The Indian Army was a constant presence in our lives in Sikkim. Its headquarters was at 17th Mile on the way to Nathu La, the border between India and China. Their barracks were kept warm by bukharis. For them, visiting civilised places like Gangtok was a real luxury. They would often stop by our house, which was directly on their route, for a game of bridge, have a meal and then move on to 17th Mile, ready to face the hardships again. But they never complained and tried to remain cheerful through the drudgery. They would listen to music, sing, play cards and keep their morale high. If we learnt anything from the army in the four years that we spent in this Himalayan kingdom, it was to face adversity with a smile. Playing bridge became a regular pastime, which also created bonds between the army and the Political Office.

The Political Officer often invited the Chogyal and palace officials for both official and informal dinners. If any dignitary came from India—which was very often—he would be invited to a spate of parties thrown by the palace as well as the Political Office.

The General Officer Commanding (GOC) of the 17 Mountain Division would also be invited for these parties, and in turn, he would invite the same crowd to the Army Institute in Gangtok, on special occasions. It was a non-family station for the army.

The Political Office had to balance the relationship between the Chogyal and the Nepalese community. The Chogyal might have been nursing ambitions for independence for Sikkim, yet there was enough opposition from within. The Political Office often played mediator and was busy being the umpire of the situation, which could flare up at any time.

As members of the Political Office, we had the privilege of going to Nathu La, braving the precarious road and fog conditions. We even saw a Chinese guard up close while he was looking at us through his binoculars.

We visited the famous Changu Lake, which was frozen. The locals believed that whenever a calamity was about to occur, Changu Lake would have a black circle in it, foreshadowing the impending events. We were told that before the Chogyal's first wife died, Changu Lake indeed had a large black circle in it. She had left behind two sons and a daughter.

The Chogyal married an American lady called Hope Cooke, who was known as the Gyalmo. He was obviously enamoured by Western culture. Although the queen wore bakus and tried to follow Bhutia traditions, the presence of American culture was palpable. A number of American visitors used to visit the palace. She brought several Anglo-Indians into the Sikkimese government, known for their close ties with her, and subtly promoted American culture. She spoke in hushed tones to mask her American accent. Her two children from the Chogyal were growing up in a mixed cultural environment, symbolising harmony.

The Sikkimese youth connected with the palace were quite taken in by the Gyalmo's Western influence and were keen to emulate her. Halloween was one such American festival that was followed with gusto by the young people. One Halloween celebration, the memory of which has stayed with us, was indeed surreal.

For us, it was like any other evening. After winding up for the day and settling into our nightwear, we were fast asleep. Suddenly, there was a thud on the main door, so loud that we woke up with a startle. Our domestic help, Tulsi, hurried to open the door. The sound of drums beating outside grew louder. Sudhir came out of the room in his dressing gown, to check what the commotion was about.

Just then Tulsi came in, repeating 'Sir, Sir, Sir' with so much excitement that he was unable to speak further. Without waiting for him to explain, Sudhir went to the drawing room. Before he knew what was happening, the Gyalmo caught hold of him and started dancing with him to the beat of the music, so did the rest of the young crowd that was accompanying her. Tulsi just stood there transfixed, wide-eyed and in shock. Unable to bear the deafening sounds of the drums, I also emerged from our room. I saw my husband, the First Secretary of the Political Office, dancing with the queen of Sikkim in his dressing gown—a most extraordinary sight to behold! The moment she saw me, she put my hand in my husband's and left as suddenly as she had arrived, leaving both of us speechless. The next day, this episode was the talk of the town.

The Chogyal's autocratic ways were increasingly becoming evident at the events organised by the palace. Living happily in their kingdom, little did the Chogyal and the Gyalmo realise that the seeds of democracy had already been sown and unrest was gathering momentum. Kazi Lhendup Dorji, a Bhutia leader, had emerged as the face of democracy. The common people of Sikkim, including the Bhutias, Lepchas and Nepalese, had come together under his banner; opposition to the Chogyal was mounting.

If Gangtok appeared to be normal, it was the silence before the storm. In 1973, on the king's birthday, there were anti-Chogyal demonstrations in Gangtok. Riots also broke out in west and south Sikkim. When the situation started getting out of hand, the First Secretary made visits to Gangtok, and an agreement was signed that called for early elections. The Government of India appointed a senior civil servant as the dewan to supervise the administration in Sikkim.

In 1974, for the first time, democratic elections took place for the Sikkim Assembly in which Kazi's party won a landslide victory and he became the Chief Minister. The Chogyal was still not able to see the writing on the wall. He continued to create hurdles in the administration. The situation was getting worse by the day. Things heated up to such an extent that the people of Sikkim asked for a merger with India in 1975. What happened afterwards is history.

When we went to Sikkim, we were on a foreign posting. After we left Sikkim, it was no longer one. We were witness to the writing of this page in history.

The saga never really left us.

That page of history was reopened when we revisited Sikkim forty years later. The idea of returning to the Himalayan state filled me with trepidation. It was an exciting opportunity, yet I did not want to disturb the images of a fairy-tale kingdom that had existed in my memory. Would Sikkim be the same? How could I expect it to be the same?

When my husband was invited for an official visit to Sikkim, we embarked on a journey to Gangtok, retracing the road that we had travelled decades ago. As our Jeep set off into the heart of the towering mountains, we eagerly looked at our surroundings. The road conditions had improved, but the roar of the mighty Teesta River had mellowed. Hydroelectric projects in several places along the river marred the serene landscape. There were many more vehicles on the road, navigating hair-pin bends. The threat of landslides remained, and the presence of nature all around us was just as striking as I remembered.

We had the privilege of staying at India House, which was now the residence of the governor, my husband's dear colleague. The guest suite was a new addition and the gardens were just as verdant. The Kanchenjunga soaring in the distance was as captivating as ever.

Sudhir had the opportunity to address students at a university, and he got to interact with young people. He felt very happy seeing young Sikkimese faces full of curiosity, who felt connected with the rest of India. The integration that had taken place nearly fifty years ago felt complete.

We decided to revisit Namchi in the south, where the merger movement had gained momentum in the 1970s and where Sudhir had been sent by the Political Office to assess the situation. On the way to Namchi, we passed Char Dham Temple where you could visit all the four Hindu holy places at one site. Built on a hill surrounded by nature, this temple complex has become a huge tourist draw, attracting thousands. As we drove further, we visited a tea garden we had been to forty years ago. As was the norm, the caretaker asked Sudhir to sign the visitors' book. When he opened the book and turned the pages casually, he chanced upon his own signature from the 1970s. That was a surreal experience.

Big changes had come to the small town of Gangtok. Its Mall Road was now a walking path, bordered by beautiful hanging plants and eateries. There were signs of booming construction everywhere.

One of the highlights of this trip was meeting old friends with whom we had lost touch. We reconnected with the conservator of forests, previously known as the orchid man, who we had been very friendly with during our years in Gangtok. It was a warm reunion. He was happy with the tax-free environment that had spurred business in the state.

We also met the Chogyal's half-sister, a dear friend with whom we had remained in touch over the years. She was as youthful and cheerful as I remembered her to be, and she greeted us warmly and affectionately in her modest home. She briefed us on the Chogyal's family members and their whereabouts. She told us about her daughter's project work on the history of Sikkim's merger with India, and how she was convinced this was the best outcome. This surprised us. We had still not forgotten our last meeting with the Chogyal when we bid him goodbye, just before the merger. Our posting orders had come, and we were to leave soon. We were made to wait over an hour by the same Chogyal who had always been a warm host to us, though he was just as gracious and courteous when he bid us farewell. We, of course, never saw him again.

Returning to Sikkim was like revisiting the past through a modern lens. There were vestiges of a bygone era—a familiar place and familiar people. But what was missing? The old kingdom, of course.

Calendars, Clocks and Confusion
Ethiopia

KUSUM BUDHWAR

A whispered hint of a new appointment had reached us a few months earlier, and we were thrilled at the prospect of it turning into reality. Were that to happen, it would be my husband's first job as Ambassador, and that too with barely eighteen years of service. It would also be the first time we would be setting foot on the continent of Africa. The year was 1980, and we were nearing the completion of our posting in Moscow. This exciting new assignment was going to take us to Ethiopia, an ancient land once known as Abyssinia, where the descendants of a dynasty founded by the biblical King Solomon and Queen Sheba had ruled since 950 BC until the overthrow of Emperor Haile Selassie in 1974. Historically, over centuries, India has maintained good relations with this country; as early as 1948, within a year after Independence, our diplomatic presence was established there.

The position in Addis Ababa had been vacant for only a short time when my husband's name was proposed as envoy. It is a routine procedure for a host country to take a few months to consider the recommendation before accepting and making it public knowledge. Such formality and courtesy are strictly adhered to in diplomacy. In the interim, one is well advised to prepare for the upcoming assignment. We did this diligently by all the means available to us in those days. We read the country note on living conditions issued by our ministry and consulted numerous books, either gifted or borrowed from friends, fellow diplomats or libraries. Gathering information was not as easy then as it is today. This was the pre-internet era. Google, Wikipedia and other search tools that we take for granted today did not exist then.

Once everything was ready, our orders were to proceed directly to the next station, present credentials to the head of state at the earliest and be in position to host our Republic Day reception. Thus, November 1979 saw us take off from Moscow's Sheremetyevo airport in subzero temperature and arrive at Addis Ababa's Bole airport, nine hours later, the following morning. To our amazement, although we had dropped many geographical latitudes from Moscow's fifty-five degrees north to Addis Ababa's nine degrees north, the longitude had more or less stayed constant, hence the time zone remained the same and the body clock needed no adjustment. What was gone was the bone-chilling, freezing cold, the snow-covered landscape and the grey skies; in their place came a gorgeous sunlit panorama set against a cloudless deep blue sky. The contrast could not have been more dramatic. This warm welcome was reinforced by the numerous posters proclaiming that we had arrived in the 'Land of Thirteen Months of Sunshine'. We smiled, and then smiled some more, looking forward to the time we were to spend in this beautiful new home of ours.

It did not take us long to settle in. India House, located on the prestigious main artery of the city, Bole Road, was a lovely, spacious residence built on a sizeable acreage. A formal, landscaped garden stretched along the driveway leading up to the house. Its lawn could easily hold a few hundred people and seemed perfect for hosting receptions. A grove of tall eucalyptus trees stood at the far end, under which was built a tukul, a gazebo-like wooden hut with a thatched roof. It lent a quaint, rustic charm and served as an ideal bar for parties

The high altitude of Addis Ababa at 6,500 feet, combined with its proximity to the Equator, gave the city moderate temperatures ranging between 25°C and 14°C year round. This subtropical weather with its cool highland air allowed us to use both summer and winter wardrobes, fans and fireplaces simultaneously. There were only two seasons: dry and wet. The climate was conducive to growing plants that thrived in tropical, temperate or alpine zones. Much to our delight, the India House gardens displayed a beautiful range of flowers and ornamental shrubs that happily defied the concept of zonal segregation. The residence came with staff quarters that housed families of the local help.

Each country has its own unique identity and we were to discover many interesting things about Ethiopia. To begin with, the slogan 'Land of Thirteen Months of Sunshine' that had first greeted us on arrival, which we had appreciated as smart and catchy, turned out to be true. One afternoon, while sitting in the garden enjoying the warm equatorial sun, Wolde, the houseboy, brought in mail from the letterbox. Among the envelopes were water and electricity bills due for payment. On checking them my husband was puzzled, as they were all dated 1972. Wondering why he was getting such old bills but not wanting to trash them either, he took them to his office. Just as well, for they turned out to be current bills. How could that be? How could bills from 1972 be current in 1980?

The mystery was solved when we learnt that Ethiopia followed a different calendar, not the universal Gregorian one used by the rest of the world. In 1582, when Pope Gregory introduced a new calendar which adjusted the equinox and solstice dates, Catholic and Protestant nations accepted the change, but the Orthodox did not. It took a few more centuries before the countries of the Orthodox faith were willing to discard the old Julian calendar. Greece and Turkey made the switch in 1926, but Ethiopia still marches to its own beat. Their calendar lags behind the Gregorian one by almost eight years. When asked why it was so, we were told that the Greek Orthodox Church needed time to recalculate an alternate date of Jesus's birth from the old calendar to the new. It took seven years for that proclamation to reach the Ethiopian Church from Greece via the Church of Alexandria.

The differences don't end here: the number of months in the year and the starting point of the year are also different. The Ethiopian calendar consists of thirteen months—twelve regular months of thirty days and a thirteenth month of either five or six days in a leap year. The year begins from 12 September and not the universal 1 January. Consequently, Ethiopia celebrated this millennium on 12 September 2007, and while we are in the year 2024, Ethiopia is in the year 2017.

In Ethiopia, time is also calculated differently. This is so because of its proximity to the Equator, which makes daylight hours consistent throughout the year. The sun rises at 6 a.m. and sets at 6 p.m. Thus, time is measured in two cycles. The twelve hours from sunrise to sunset are considered daytime, and the other twelve hours are nighttime. Their clock starts counting hours from sunrise, and not from midnight. Seven a.m., being the first hour after sunrise, is therefore one o'clock, 8 a.m. becomes two o'clock, and so on. Their clock face is the opposite of the analogue clock faces we are used to, with six at the top and twelve at the bottom. It may be confusing to outsiders, but is quite logical for those living near the Equator. Ethiopians are a proud, independent-minded people. Their country was never colonised, so it's unlikely that they will change either their calendar or readjust their clocks to follow the rest of the world.

As we stepped into January, preparations for the Republic Day reception gathered momentum. Invitation cards were printed keeping in mind the local calendar and time. It was necessary to mention both for the convenience of our Ethiopian invitees. An exhaustive list was prepared, covering Ambassadors, senior representatives of international organisations, prominent members of the Indian community and, of course, VIPs of the current country of accreditation. Addis Ababa had a sizeable Indian community that was much loved and respected for its contribution to the development of the country. Indians were most notable in the fields of education, medicine and trade. The diplomatic presence, too, was impressive with close to eighty missions located here. Apart from that, numerous important UN bodies, including the Food and Agriculture Organization, International Labour Organization and Organization of African Unity, maintained their headquarters here, making it an important capital city in Africa.

We were fortunate to have an excellent Indian restaurant, Sangam, not too far from our residence. Its owner, Mr Desikan, was a pleasant, friendly and accommodating person who was more than happy to take charge of the food and catering service. Since our rules forbade serving of alcohol on national day parties, a wide range of soft drinks and juices had been purchased for the occasion. The reception was planned as a late-afternoon event, scheduled from 4 p.m. to 6 p.m. This timing was ideal: the sun was no longer at its peak, but there was still daylight for another two hours before dusk. Besides, this was not the hour when people missed having a stronger drink than juice.

Come 4 p.m., the Indian Embassy officials and their wives, dressed in their formal attire of bandgala suits and silk saris, lined up to welcome the guests. As is the norm in diplomatic circles, almost everybody came on time. Soon the garden was filled with people mingling, chattering and enjoying the feast laid out for them. We joined in as well, making small talk and savouring the happy moments, but as time passed and the party neared its end, we felt a pang of disappointment, as no representative of the Ethiopian government had put in an appearance so far. Noticing this, regulars of the diplomatic circuit informed us that this was not unusual under the new military regime and we should not take it amiss. Comforted, we smiled and graciously thanked those who had attended the reception. By 6 p.m., darkness fell and only a few friends remained, chatting idly, waiting for their cars.

Seeing that the party was over, I slipped away and went indoors to thank the photographer, caterer, waiters and household staff, and to tell them to enjoy the food before clearing up. That's when I suddenly heard some commotion outside and went to look into it. There were a couple of black official-looking limousines entering the gate and slowly making their way up the driveway, and Wolde was excitedly telling my husband that the Minister of Foreign Affairs was just arriving. Soon thereafter, following the first motorcade, came another lot of similar-looking cars; this time it was the Foreign Secretary with his entourage. Hiding his astonishment and leaving the group he was conversing with, my husband stepped forward to warmly welcome the latecomers, privately wondering if there had been some confusion about the time given.

My first reaction to these rapidly unfolding events was that of any housewife. Oh my God! Immediately, I made a dash for the kitchen, unceremoniously grabbed the platters of food I had just moments ago given away so generously and ordered that they be saved and served to the new arrivals. The now relaxing waiters were summoned to attention. The photographer, who was on his way home, was contacted and asked to return at once and Mr Desikan was requested to send more food and snacks. Only then did I return to join the guests.

By now it was dark outdoors and a chill had set in so the Ethiopian dignitaries were invited to come indoors and get comfortable in the drawing room. And there they all were, chatting amiably with my husband. Setting the tone for the evening, he announced merrily that the official reception was now over and everyone could order a drink of their choice. The atmosphere changed immediately, all formality dropped and a spirit of bonhomie filled the room. Tandoori chicken, mutton kebabs, fish fingers, samosas, etc., accompanied by cognac, whisky and beer added to the good cheer. What a jolly evening it turned out to be! It was late into the night when we finally saw off our guests. By the following day, word had spread like wildfire through the diplomatic corps as to who all had come to India House to greet the Ambassador on India's national day. The phone rang incessantly. Colleagues from our diplomatic circle wanted to know how we had managed to swing such a coup so soon, while others called simply to congratulate us on such an unheard-of success. My husband laughed heartily, filled with pride.

An interesting aside to the evening was that during a conversation with the foreign minister, my husband mentioned that the first article he ever wrote for his college magazine, back in the 1950s, was about Ethiopia. While in college, he had an Ethiopian classmate who had come to India as a student for higher studies on a Government of India scholarship. Since they became good friends, my husband often asked him questions about his country and that information formed the basis of the article. Recalling the name of his friend, Tessima Ibido, he asked the foreign minister whether he could somehow locate him in case he was still around. To the astonishment of all, the minister revealed that he knew Tessima Ibido personally and mentioned that he had done well in life, recently retiring as their deputy finance minister. He assured us that he would convey the message and ask him to get in touch. Within a couple of days, Tessima called and came over to our home. What a warm meeting it was between the friends! The clock stood still as they reminisced about the happy days of their youth spent together in Shimla.

Thereafter, for the rest of our stay in Ethiopia, Tessima would often visit us or we him. Once he invited us to join him for a fasting meal. Intrigued by such an invitation, we accepted. My, what an eye-opener that was! I knew that people of the Orthodox faith fasted twice a week, on Wednesdays and Fridays. Out of consideration, I kept the housework light for the staff on those days, thinking they might be low on energy. But after this fasting lunch, it was clear that I need not have worried. The table groaned under the weight of the dishes—vegetables, lentils, fruits and even fish. Incredulously, I turned to my host and asked how one could eat all this and still claim to be fasting. He looked at me with a twinkle in his eye and said, 'Hah! But there is no meat, eggs or any dairy products!'

Another relationship that enriched our posting was our friendship with Afewerk Tekle. A suave, handsome man who spoke fluent English, he introduced us to the art and culture of his country. He was a brilliant trendsetting artist, who was highly regarded both in his country and internationally. Tekle was the first African whose portrait was acquired by the renowned Uffizi Gallery in Florence as part of its permanent collection, and upon whom France conferred the title of Honourable World Laureate Maitre Artist. He had studied art at the prestigious Slade School of Fine Art, London, and travelled extensively through Europe and

Africa, honing his skills. His artworks occupy a place of honour in Ethiopia and are treasured as national heritage. His masterpieces include the 'Maskal Flower', 'Mother Ethiopia' and numerous others spread over five decades. These decades saw his country go through turbulent times, including three dramatic regime changes. First came the Italian occupation (1936–1941), lasting five years, followed by a return to imperial rule under Emperor Haile Selassie. During this period, Afewerk, already an established artist, enjoyed royal patronage and its attendant privileges as a courtier. The painting *Maskal Flower* captures the essence of this era. It is a full-length portrait of a strikingly beautiful young lady of nobility, dressed in rich clothing, casually holding a yellow daisy, the Maskal flower. In Afewerk's personal life, it was a time of unrequited love and heartbreak.

In 1974, Emperor Selassie was overthrown in a revolution and a Communist military junta government came to power. As is the norm, every new regime carries out purges against people associated with the previous ruler; Afewerk was not spared. By 1980, the worst of these purges were over, and thousands of political and other prisoners were released from jails and reinstated. The Ministry of Education and Culture asked Afewerk's help in formulating a new policy for the country. It was in this capacity that we first met him in Ethiopia.

What gave our friendship a boost was an idea we implemented together. It so happened that soon after our arrival in Addis Ababa, two young people representing Vikas Publishing House came to explore the African market for academic books published in India. I suggested that as an introduction we conduct a children's on-the-spot painting competition. I would invite the master artist to conduct and judge the competition. That idea was a grand success and became an annual feature. What's more, the two young men went on to become publishers in their own right; Narender

Kumar started Har Anand and K.P.R. Nair founded Konark. Soon, we became close enough to Afewerk to share personal stories and enjoy each other's hospitality. He had never been to India, so at our recommendation he was invited as an honoured guest to meet Prime Minister Indira Gandhi. The call on Mrs Gandhi, which was scheduled for fifteen minutes, lasted close to an hour!

Before we left Addis Ababa, Afewerk invited us to a private dinner at his villa. We were keen to buy one of his paintings, and he agreed to our request. That evening, he took us on a tour of his studio and asked us to select a painting. We looked at the lovely pieces, but we wanted more—something we had admired and associated with him from earlier visits. My husband looked at him and asked softly, 'Afewerk, all these are beautiful, but I would really like to buy the picture that hangs above your bed, that first study of the Maskal Flower.' Afewerk was taken aback at this unexpected request and fell into a long silence. After a while, he nodded and said, 'Alright, it is yours. Since you know the story connected to it and you are aware how dear and meaningful it is to me, I am at ease knowing it remains in safe custody. However, there is a stipulation. If I have an exhibition where it is required, then it must come back for that purpose.' We agreed to his terms and he signed it over to us. It remains a proud possession and a memory of the happy times spent together. Afewerk Tekle passed away in 2012, aged seventy-nine.

Our travels in Ethiopia were exciting but erratic due to insurgency in certain parts of the country. Its cultural history lay in antiquity, so there was much on offer.

Lalibela, regarded as one of the wonders of the world, opened briefly during a lull in fighting, and we were permitted to visit the site. It is famed for its rock-hewn monolithic churches, which use a technique similar to that of the Kailasa Temple in Ellora. These eleven churches date back to eleventh and twelfth centuries and are a sacred pilgrimage site. Unsafe conditions were apparent from the moment our plane landed. The radar guiding it was mounted on a moving van, and as soon as the aircraft came to a halt, the van drove off with the pilot and crew, taking all the precious equipment with it. Everyone else left using various modes of transport, leaving just the two of us sitting on our bags under a thatched roof, waiting for our taxi and guide. However, on seeing those rock-cut marvels, all else was forgotten.

We also visited the old fortified city of Harar, once a bustling hub on the Arab trade route. There, we saw three interesting things: a strange-looking striped donkey, which turned out to be a zebroid—a cross between a zebra and a donkey; a photo in a shop window of a hyena man; and old Indian coins being sold in the market. Of course, we bought a few.

The hyena man intrigued us, so we arranged a viewing in exchange for a bucket of meat. After dark we went to a forested area on the outskirts of town and sat silently in our car, observing. After a while, the man came and sat in a clearing on the forest floor. He began to hum and sway, calling out names in a sing-song voice. Suddenly, from the shadows, hyenas started to approach him. He fed each one a chunk of meat he held in his mouth. When all the meat was finished, he bade them to leave. How incredible and eerie that was!

From Harar we returned to Addis Ababa by train. Even that turned out to be quite an experience. Our companions were ordinary folk with their livestock of goats, sheep and chickens. There were stops along the way when the entire train would empty onto the nearby fields so people and animals alike could stretch their legs before reaching the station. It was hilarious.

There is much to tell when you travel and observe keenly. In Bahir Dar, we saw the great Lake Tana, where papyrus boats from biblical times still ply between forbidding-looking monasteries. We saw the ribbon-like Blue Nile emerge from the lake, and almost fifty kilometres later, transform into the spectacular Tissisat Falls. We tasted honey wine in village shops and drank coffee in its original home, the Kaffa province.

I'll end with our visit to Keren, a town now in Eritrea. In 1983, Indian naval ships made a goodwill gesture and docked at the port of Massawa. The captain requested a visit to the war cemetery in Keren, about a hundred and fifty kilometres away. Insurgency was at its peak in Eritrea, which was then fighting for its independence from Ethiopia. The Ministry of Defence was reluctant to put our lives at risk, but at our insistence they somehow arranged for us to be flown there in army helicopters and heightened security. During the Second World War, in 1941, Indian troops in the British Army were sent to fight in this region.

When I saw the terrain where the battle took place, it smote my heart; it was a hopeless position to be fighting from. The enemy had all the advantages, and our boys had none. All 285 names of those who died there are inscribed on the commemorative panel in the cemetery. The average age of our soldiers was between twenty-four and thirty years. Buglers from our navy played *The Last Post*, and we laid down wreaths in honour of our brave heroes. It is moment I will never forget, one that still gives me a lump in the throat.

In conclusion, I'd say that as the wife of a diplomat, I always walked in step with my husband and took my role as a representative of my country equally seriously. Diplomatic life comes with privileges and trials of its own; while not every posting is a cakewalk, many are. My own life in the foreign service began in war-torn Vietnam, and I recall my young husband assuring me then that life could only get better after this. And it did. The mantra for enjoying this nomadic life is to accept, adapt and assimilate.

My Life in the Rainbow Nation
South Africa

KUSUM TAYAL

One fine day in August 1995, while working at the public-sector bank where I had been employed for about six years, I received a call from my husband, Skand. We were expecting our posting abroad after five long years in India and the ministry grapevine had it that we were going to Washington. I was excited and had already started dreaming about life in America, thinking this was the moment I had been waiting for. But Skand's telephone call left me in tears. Not knowing what had transpired, my colleagues in the bank were puzzled. We were going to Africa instead of America, I told them. They sympathised with me. Over the landline, my husband tried his best to explain to me that his posting to Johannesburg in South Africa was as Consul General and head of post, whereas in Washington he would have just been one of the many officers in a large embassy. My initial unhappiness about being posted to South Africa gradually faded over the course of three adventurous years in that beautiful land.

My husband's posting as Consul General in Johannesburg was during the period when Nelson Mandela, recently released from prison, was leading the nation after decades of apartheid. During our stay, from December 1995 to December 1998, we witnessed historic transformation in a racially divided country.

This was just the beginning of my taking an extended leave of absence from my work to be a trailing diplomatic spouse. I realise I must be one of the very few fortunate foreign service wives who have managed to hold on to their original careers. My employer, a public-sector bank, was understanding and generous in granting me leave without pay. After my husband retired from service, I was able to rejoin the bank, though at the same scale-II manager grade level. I sometimes look back with some envy at a scale-I probationary officer who had worked under me in a branch and went on to become the managing director in a nationalised bank, while I was still working at the same grade-II level. I have no regrets over my decision, as I got to see the world—a chance very few get. We, from the foreign service fraternity, often take this for granted and grumble at every inconvenience, but there is struggle in whichever path one pursues in life. Had I continued with my banking career, I, too, would have had to shift houses to various cities in India, facing multiple other challenges.

Now, many years later, I appreciate how fortunate we were to get posted to South Africa during the era of the iconic Nelson Mandela. Here was a man on whom the hopes of an entire nation were pinned, who was inspired by Mahatma Gandhi and had spent twenty-seven years of his life in a tiny cell in the notorious Robben Island prison. Gandhi-ji had spent twenty-one years in South Africa, from 1893 to 1914, and his message of non-violence and peace still resonates in the rainbow country. The Indian South African community constitutes only about 2.5 per cent of the total population of sixty million, yet it is active in every sphere and also contributes to preserving Gandhi-ji's legacy. We made a few trips to Tolstoy Farm, about some thirty-odd kilometres from Johannesburg, where Gandhi-ji experimented with communal living between 1910 and 1914. Unfortunately, the farmhouse was repeatedly vandalised every time it was restored by the generous efforts of Indian South Africans. My father had regaled us children with stories of how he had participated in several marches in support of Gandhi-ji and had burnt foreign-made clothes in Mangalore during his youth. I was curious to see how Mandela, who was an ideological successor to Gandhi-ji, would be like up close.

President Mandela is revered the world over, even more so after his passing away in 2013. Initially, the West dismissed Mandela as a communist and the African National Congress (ANC) was labelled a terrorist organisation, but now the world acknowledges what an incredible man he was. The transformation of an unjust and unequal society does not happen unless bold and visionary steps are undertaken by the leaders of the nation.

To bring closure to those who had suffered brutalities at the hands of the oppressive white regime in South Africa, which enforced apartheid for decades, President Mandela established the Truth and Reconciliation Commission (TRC). The goal of TRC was to heal the wounds of injustice by having the aggressors appear before the commission to narrate and repent their actions in the presence of their victims. The court-like commission, chaired by Nobel laureate Archbishop Desmond Tutu, emphasised encouraging both perpetrators and victims to reveal the truth, with the understanding that there would be no prosecution for the atrocities committed during the apartheid period. This unique approach was radically different from other commissions held worldwide. The focus was on reconciliation rather than retribution. This helped the racially divided society to continue to coexist in the new South Africa without much acrimony.

An embassy colleague's wife, who was more adventurous than me, called one day and asked if I would like to accompany her for one of the hearings at the TRC. My husband was sceptical, unsure if it was appropriate for an Indian envoy's wife to attend such hearings. But curiosity got the better of me, and I, along with my friend, went on a Monday morning to the commission courthouse. Winnie Mandela was attending that session during which a white South African policeman recalled in detail how he had brutalised defenceless Black people several years ago. Winnie Mandela sat quietly, expressionless behind big dark glasses; one could not guess what she was thinking at that moment. Was she remembering all the torture, insults, grief and pain that her fellow Black South Africans had to endure during the apartheid days? Also, I wondered, what were the thoughts running through President Mandela's mind when he read the headlines in the South African press every day, reporting these traumatic recollections of his countrymen. The third day of the hearing was particularly haunting, when the brutality against a fifteen-year-old child was narrated by an Afrikaner, a South African of Dutch ancestry. I came out of the room with tears flowing down my cheeks, unable to comprehend how cruel someone could be to a fellow human being.

I now realise the significance of this commission, which was so unlike the Nuremberg trials, conducted to seek retribution and punishment for the atrocities committed by the Nazis. Racism is an issue that one can encounter anywhere, even in today's world. When we were finally posted to the country I was initially so excited about, the United States, I would personally witness its ugly form. In Houston, Texas, our eleven-year-old son was traumatised, as he was repeatedly taunted as 'Paki' by an American child in school.

I was shocked and couldn't imagine this happening to my own son. I had thought we diplomats were a privileged lot, yet here was my eleven-year-old being racially bullied. However, when I brought this to the attention of the class teacher, the matter was immediately taken up with the seriousness it deserved. The parents of that American child were called to the school and the matter was discussed with them. Ultimately, the child apologised to our son. But now, back to our South African days.

After decades of injustice, transformation does not happen overnight. Years of apartheid and denial of education have resulted in more than 35 per cent unemployment among Black people. Poverty and broken families have led to a high crime rate in the country, particularly in Johannesburg. One incident just three months after our arrival left us quite shaken. It was early March 1996, and the springtime weather was beautiful. I, along with my children, arrived at a birthday party of a colleague's daughter who was staying in Rosebank, an affluent suburb just around five kilometres from our residence. My husband came straight from the office around 6 p.m. in his official Mercedes car. His chauffeur, David, who had been with the Consulate for a while, was an efficient and careful driver. My husband got out of the car and David was searching for parking, as it was a very busy street with cars parked along the curb. About five minutes after my husband arrived at the apartment, there was a commotion at the door. A flustered, out-of-breath David came rushing in. He was incoherent. It turned out that while he was looking for parking, a car pulled up and four men with automatic guns stepped out. One of them put a gun against David's temple and demanded the car keys. David fumbled but handed over the keys. After which, two of the men got into the Mercedes and disappeared. Just like that. Our car had been hijacked.

Skand immediately contacted Sharma Maharaj, the Johannesburg police commissioner, who was of Indian origin. He took down the details of the car, which were immediately flashed all over the city. However, he gave us little hope, as this was a common way for miscreants and jobless people to make money. Later, we learnt that we were fortunate our chauffeur David was a Black South African, or else he might have been shot. We made a conscious decision then, and I bought a nondescript Honda Accord, which we would use to drive to places that were considered unsafe.

The company that was entrusted with the security of the residence and the Consulate building insisted that we keep a panic button with us at all times when we were home. Not only was this most inconvenient but it also constantly reminded us of lurking trouble. Several mock drills were conducted to get to the panic room in the basement within two minutes. Our bedrooms on the first floor had iron grills, and at night we were all 'caged' and locked in. Every evening, it felt as if we were imprisoned in a cage, while robbers and thieves had free rein to roam the city and do as they pleased. It was disconcerting and did not feel like a normal life. After a couple of months, we gave up on the panic button, but made sure we were careful while coming out of the house or driving to any place. The hijacked official car was eventually found two years later in Zimbabwe, riddled with bullet holes. Sadly enough, we were to experience another incident of carjacking during our three-year stint. It happened a few months before we left the country. While visiting a hospital to see a colleague who was seriously ill, four Consulate wives and I were nonplussed when we realised that the Consulate van which had dropped us at the hospital was nowhere to be found when we returned. The next day, we learnt that the Consulate driver had stolen the van and disappeared! Fortunately, this time the van was found after a week and rumours were that the driver had stolen it to buy smack. In just one posting, we had experienced two different incidents of carjacking.

There was no dearth of strange occurrences in Johannesburg. It had always been my dream to do two things: learn to play the piano and ride a horse. I was not so sure if learning horse riding in my middle age was a great idea, but I was keen to fulfil the first dream. And lo and behold, I met a young Indian expat wife who was proficient in playing the veena but was game to learn the piano. We came across an advertisement in the local newspaper of a young Russian pianist offering piano lessons at his home. When we arrived at the given address, it turned out to be a large private house. The Russian teacher took us to the back of the house, where our piano lessons began twice a week—on Tuesdays and Thursdays. It was exciting to have realised a childhood dream. My friend had a keyboard at home, so she would practise before class. I also needed to practise, so my teacher helped us choose and buy a second-hand German piano. I am so thankful to him because thirty years later I continue to play Bach and Beethoven on that very piano.

One Tuesday morning, about four months after our piano classes had started, we arrived at the house as usual, only to find the backdoor locked with no sign of any inhabitants. We were puzzled, rang the bell and tried to open the door, but it was locked. We then went to the front of the house, where a strange man answered and claimed that it was his house and no other person lived there! When we tried to explain about our piano teacher, who had taught us there for four months, he said he knew nothing about it. As two young women from a foreign country, we did not want to probe further and hurriedly left the place. It was quite a strange experience, and I still think about it after so many years. Although I later found another South African piano teacher, we would often speculate about what happened to our young Russian piano teacher. As an avid fan of spy and crime movies, I can't help but suspect he was a drug dealer!

Now let me tell you about my first 'meeting' with President Mandela. It happened in May 1996 during the funeral of a veteran ANC leader who had been tortured, beaten and locked up during the apartheid era for demanding equal rights for the Black people. Hundreds of people had gathered, and suddenly there was a lot of chattering and excitement. There are very few people whose entry completely changes the energy of a room or space; Mandela was definitely one of them. When I looked in that direction, I found him standing just ten feet away from us. Slowly, the music started and dancing began—yes, dancing at a funeral! That is the African custom: when someone dies, you celebrate their life. So, to my utter shock, instead of sadness and solemnity, there was singing and dancing. President Mandela was also an excellent dancer. I think it is an inborn talent in Africans; there is a rhythm and gracefulness to them as they enjoy life.

Our visits to Cape Town, one of the most beautiful cities in the world, were memorable in many ways. The city has everything—the sea, mountains, greenery, wineries and stunning views wherever you go. But a trip to the infamous Robben Island prison is also a must. It's humbling to think that an inspiring, educated leader like Mandela was trapped in a cell for so many years simply for advocating equal rights for all South Africans. After decades of struggle and being called a terrorist, Mandela was released, and in the 1994 elections, the ANC won a landslide victory. However, President Mandela was prepared to forgive the apartheid regime's past oppression to build a new South Africa.

We had quite a few other incredible experiences in South Africa. Our visit to an ostrich farm near Cape Town was one such adventure. The unique experience was a ride on the back of an ostrich. The trick was to cover the bird's head with a black scarf, which confuses the bird somewhat, so it sits still. Once you climb onto its back, the ostrich handler makes it stand up. When the scarf is removed from the ostrich's head, that's when the fireworks begin. In my case, the bird took off with me desperately clutching its back to avoid toppling over. But ultimately, it was the bird that won. I was thrown off its back, landing gently thanks to the handler who ran alongside us. Everybody in the family was roaring with laughter at this most hilarious sight!

Another unforgettable experience was thanks to our High Commissioner, Gopalkrishna Gandhi, grandson of Mahatma Gandhi. He and his wife were invited to the coronation of King Letsie III of Lesotho on 31 October 1997, as India's High Commissioner to South Africa is concurrently accredited to Lesotho. A small independent country, Lesotho is landlocked by South Africa. As they were expecting royalty from all over the world, their foreign office asked all Ambassadors and High Commissioners to make their own private arrangements for travel within the country. High Commissioner Gandhi asked Skand if we would be willing to travel by road in his official car to Maseru, the capital of Lesotho. We gladly accepted. Thus, we were to witness firsthand the coronation of a king. Prince Charles (now King Charles III) and his son Harry attended the event, sitting two rows behind us. Prince Charles looked rather bored. For us, it was a special honour to witness this unique occasion; for him, it must have been one of the many mundane chores and business as usual. The ceremony followed tribal customs in an open sports stadium. King Letsie was escorted into the venue by mounted police carrying sabres and lances. He was crowned in a traditional tribal ceremony by two chieftains. The crown was a beaded headband adorned with brown and white feathers. This ceremony stood in stark contrast to the coronation of

King Charles III in Britain on 6 May 2023, which was telecast all over the world. King Letsie III was one the guests at King Charles's coronation.

All our postings were unique, with different societies, living conditions and challenges. I made lasting friends in each of those countries. Life as a foreign service spouse brings massive upheaval every three years. Ultimately, it is both the people and the experiences that make a place memorable. Keeping my career helped me have my unique perspective on each country we were posted to. It helped me appreciate the opportunities each posting offered. Hence, the hat of 'trailing diplomatic spouse' is one that I would very happily take if I had to choose all over again.

Beyond the Smoke that Thunders
Zimbabwe

MARGRETA KUMAR

A car approached the driveway. I heard a door slam shut and an exchange of voices. I continued to concentrate on the dining table. I had to make sure that all the arrangements were impeccable for the social evening.

A voice suddenly said, 'It's Zimbab way!'

I looked up.

'What way?' I quipped, feeling annoyed by this habit of men wanting to poke their noses into what a woman was doing.

My husband sensed my confusion.

'I am going as the Ambassador to Zimbabwe!' he announced.

I stopped short of perfecting the floral arrangement on the table, moved towards him and, with a peck on his cheek, said, 'Congratulations!'

We had actually just returned a day ago from a quick sightseeing trip to Victoria Falls.

And so begins this journey ... Hop, skip and jump over the border! No crossing of continents and oceans, waiting months for baggage to arrive and family to settle down. This should be a piece of cake, with the hope that, after protocols and permits were met, our belongings would arrive in no time along with our four-legged furry friends: Duke, our labrador, and Zac, our teddy hamster. And they promptly did, by road!

At the animal pick-up centre, a curious Zimbabwean officer pointed a finger at Zac and queried what species the animal was.

'Rat!' retorted my husband.

I thought crecitus, cricitus or just rattus would have had a softer sound to it.

India House, the much-hyped embassy residence, sat on a sprawling eighteen-acre plot of land in one of Harare's best residential areas, Borrowdale. While the house itself was closer to the road, the back garden was the size of a few football fields. It was almost like having one's own private safari park in the backyard. However, much to our disappointment, not all was in order. My spirits were dampened. The house was in a dilapidated state, with leaking roofs on all sides and furnishings destroyed beyond repair. Everything would need extensive repairs and replacements to make it habitable. This meant we would have to wait for our ministry to approve financial sanctions to start renovations. It was a waiting game that would slow down the settling in process.

After a few months, while repair works were gaining momentum, from the bedroom window I suddenly noticed thick smoke bellowing at the far end of the backyard. And before we realised what was happening, a wild fire had begun to spread rapidly through the field. The staff residing on the premises ran helter skelter, finding ways to douse the fire with banana leaves, old trousers, blankets and buckets of water. I remembered the swimming pool and shouted that they should get water from there quickly. The fire brigade arrived promptly—but with empty tankers! The firemen, in a most apologetic manner, confessed they had no water to fill them. This was pathetic! The field was reduced to ashes thanks to the neighbours who were enjoying a braii, or barbeque, that afternoon and didn't realise a live splinter had flown over the fence into our yard. Since that day, my husband made sure that the wild areas behind the house were always mowed.

A few weeks into a posting comes the first and most formal protocol for every Ambassador: presenting his credentials to the head of state. The president's palace had requested a rehearsal before the actual formal ceremony. We were instructed on how to approach the president, what pace to walk at, how to bow—neither too low nor too high—how to shake hands and how to greet. The drill was repeated several times until they felt we had got it right. By that time, I, for one, was ready to meet the Queen of England if the opportunity ever arose in the future.

President Robert Mugabe was kind enough to invite our children, who were aged thirteen and eleven at the time. As we were ushered into the formal lounge room, he proudly pointed at Africa's Big Five—lion, kudu, elephant, leopard, rhinoceros—and a collection of other skeletal heads with glowing beady eyes hanging on the walls of the palace hall, looking menacingly at spectators.

'Are you not afraid of them?' President Mugabe asked my children.

'No, they are dead!' my son simply replied.

The president seemed amused and let out a soft chuckle.

We spent a good forty-five minutes conversing over a cup of tea. What amazed me was his profound intelligence, sharp memory and amazing sense of humour. At times, I was afraid to laugh too much or too loudly, so I maintained my poise as best as I could.

India and Zimbabwe enjoyed a cordial relationship. When the latter gained independence in 1980, India's Prime Minister Indira Gandhi attended the Independence Day ceremony. President Mugabe was also known as a reconciliator, having allowed the former White ruler, Ian Smith, to stay on as an ordinary farmer and continue receiving his pension. These were the golden years of Zimbabwean independence. However, President Mugabe ensured that his rival for power, Joshua Nkomo—whose faction India had supported—was removed.

In 2003, a new opposition party, the Movement of Democratic Change (MDC), led by Morgan Tsvangirai, gained popularity. President Mugabe saw it as being propped up by White farmers. To please the veterans of the independence war, the president adopted controversial land reforms, resulting in several generations of White farmers being removed from their properties. Consequently, Zimbabwe's economy collapsed as large-scale commercial farms were taken over by the ministers and Mugabe loyalists. The severity of hyperinflation and institutional corruption turned the bread basket of southern Africa into a basket case.

The situation worsened as the European Union and USA imposed sanctions on Zimbabwe. Food items and basic necessities became scarce. People had to deal with millions of Zimbabwean dollars, and even the counting machines soon stopped working. The people of Zimbabwe went through harrowing times and there was an exodus of refugees to South Africa. India donated 50,000 tonnes of rice at one point during a drought. Additionally, India utilised the five million dollars sanctioned for small and medium sized enterprises in Zimbabwe by bringing local people to India for training and providing agricultural machinery to their country.

Interestingly, Gujarati-origin Zimbabweans revealed that they made 200 per cent profit during the apartheid era and 100 per cent profit during this difficult Mugabe era.

Zimbabwe, an Eden of contrasts, has Harare as its capital, often called 'The Pearl of Africa'. The city has tall buildings and abundant green spaces, with flamboyant jacaranda trees lining the streets—a sight to behold during spring. Harare also enjoys one of the most pleasant and delightful climates in the world. The country is home to many hidden gems. Victoria Falls, Africa's mightiest waterfall and one of the wonders of the world, is best viewed from the Zimbabwean side. The locals call it 'Mosi-oa-Tunya', meaning 'The Smoke that Thunders'. It is a combination of five falls that are twice as tall as the Niagara Falls and span one and a half times its width. Clouds of vapour rise up to seventy metres and a cascade of five hundred million litres of water thunders into the depths of the gorge. It looks terrifying yet mesmerising at the same time. As one walks around this magical, unspoilt wonder, one gets drenched by curtains of spray, making it impossible to take photographs. Each time Victoria Falls acquires new dimensions, showcasing its myriad personality with the changing seasons. A rainbow arches perennially over the falls.

Hwange National Park is the largest wildlife reserve in the region. It was once a major wildlife resort with over a hundred species of birds and animals, including zebras, giraffes, hippos, steenboks and elephants. It is not uncommon to see white rhinos up close and personal. River cruises on the Zambezi River are a must for birdwatchers and sunset lovers. Matobo National Park offers a scenery of hills, unique rock faces and boulders piled on top of each other like building blocks. Located southeast of Harare, Matopos National Park features remarkable Stone Age rock formations. Interestingly, these balancing rocks are depicted on every Zimbabwean banknote as symbols of stability and peace.

A pretty little tourist town called Nyanga, famous for golf and fishing, is set among soft rolling hills dotted with waterfalls. There is a wooden stone house called Tony's Coffee Shop nestled in the greenery, known for its delicious pastries and coffee—a favourite with visitors. The town of Masvingo is also worth mentioning. It comprises the largest prehistoric ruins south of the Sahara and was once a powerful centre of international trade. Another must-mention is Leopard Rock in Vumba, a resort and golf course that was once considered the best in southern Africa, but whose upkeep has significantly deteriorated. It once had spectacular fairways and greens carved into a landscape of breathtaking grandeur. In spite of the harsh economic conditions affecting the maintenance of these gems, Zimbabwe still remains a song and a spell that binds all those who know her.

Zimbabwe used to boast the highest literacy rate in Sub-Saharan Africa. English is the country's lingua franca used in government and business, and is the main medium of instruction in Harare's many schools. Every educational institution takes pride in upholding high standards and shaping well-rounded individuals. Children from the diplomatic corps and local elite studied at the Harare International School. Having lived in South Africa for three years, my children were not sure what to expect when we moved to Zimbabwe in 2003. Since they were neighbouring countries, they expected some similarities. While many things seemed familiar—the weather, the stunning nature and people—there was, however, a huge difference due to the economic situation and lack of a thriving commercial presence in Harare. For starters, there were no foreign brands, products or franchises in the country. My children seemed shattered to find there was no McDonald's, no video games for their consoles as they weren't sold in any stores, and no amusement parks or arcades to visit. Instead, they ended up learning horse riding. Their lifestyle was going to be different.

As time went by, they adapted, as everyone does, and started getting used to the daily life there while continuing to encounter unique experiences. A particularly memorable moment was when they wanted to eat chocolate ice cream one day. I went to the shop to buy a store-brand carton labelled 'chocolate', only to discover after opening it that it was pink in colour and tasted more like strawberry with traces of chocolate! This disappointment lingered; a couple of months later I found my daughter flipping through my recipe books. A recipe for chocolate ice cream caught her eye. She had never cooked before, let alone make ice cream, so she asked if we could buy the ingredients together. Of course, we had to order the ice cream–making machine first. In no time, my daughter had painstakingly made the most delicious flavourful chocolate ice cream we had ever tasted. This was the beginning of the small joys of life in Zimbabwe! Her ice cream was served and appreciated at some of our dinners, which provided a motivational push for her to keep exploring her talent.

Then there were times when our house experienced power outages for hours at a time and we had to light candles to be able to see in the dark. Not having electricity meant not being able to watch TV, but as a family we played paper games by candlelight to entertain ourselves and pass the time. Spending quality time together was irreplaceable and something we all look back on fondly. The children realised that it wasn't so bad that there was no fast food available, because it meant we cooked together and ate healthy meals. We even grew our own produce, such as strawberries, tomatoes, chillies, herbs, etc. It didn't matter that there were no theme parks because children of other embassy officials and friends always got together to bond and play outdoors, letting their imaginations soar beyond expectations. My son developed leadership skills and concentrated on sports and music. He even formed a boy band and took part in the Harare International Festival of the Arts, where artists come to participate from all over the world. The band won the competition in their category! There seemed to be a bigger overarching lesson that, I believe, they learnt: In life, it isn't about where you are and what you do, but rather *who* you are with. When you share your life with people who love and support you, all the challenges of life, big and small, become easier to face. In any challenging posting, life throws up many difficult moments, and as parents, we can only provide support, love and encouragement to young minds. We can transform them by creating learning opportunities or making fun memories with the hope that these challenges will help our children face the future with more confidence and wisdom.

Zimbabweans are truly humble and dedicated people. Despite the hyperinflation and tough conditions, their resilience was unbelievable. They would queue for hours to buy bread without a single complaint. When petrol was in short supply, both men and women queued overnight, and even for days, sleeping in their vehicles, waiting for their turn to fill up their tanks. If there was one thing to learn from them, it was patience. There is no describing the plight of the local people. In Harare, we women formed several social groups with active participating members. Notably, there was the Indian Women's Association, where the spouse of the Indian head of mission automatically became the president. The committee members worked together to strengthen the bond within the Indian community through cultural programmes but, most of all, to assist the local people through our charity initiatives.

Then there was the Asian Diplomatic Ladies' Group. As its president in 2005, I helped organise monthly coffee mornings on a rotational basis. Our goal was to discuss and share ideas for upcoming agendas and to focus on raising funds to help the underprivileged people of Zimbabwe. Our Asian evening was a highly anticipated event among the diplomatic corps and elites of Harare. During this event, all Asian diplomatic missions would contribute one or two national dishes, organise cultural shows and put up exhibits of art and craft. There were sport competitions, lottery tickets and more. The proceeds from ticket sales would go into helping local village schools, old age homes, orphans of AIDS patients, and the sick and disabled.

There were over thirty-two foreign missions and international organisations in Harare. Being a sizeable diplomatic community, we formed the Diplomatic Spouses' Association (DSA), for which I served as president in 2005. Selected committee members would meet monthly for brainstorming sessions. We had various clubs, such as cooking, painting, mahjong, tennis, Pilates, that welcomed anyone to join by paying a small membership fee. Football tournaments were organised for Ambassadors, who had to pay to play. We sold DSA T-shirts and food to spectators. We also compiled a cookbook with international recipes, which was sold to raise funds for charity.

We often made weekly visits to homes, schools, villages and clinics to assess their genuine needs after receiving requests for assistance, which mostly included medicines, blankets, clothes, food, toys, chalks, pencils, books and baby formula, or sometimes support for installing toilets, water tanks, taps in schools, classroom benches and so on. We also distributed food weekly to orphaned children left in the care of old grandparents with no financial means to support them. It was most heart-wrenching to witness babies and young children going through such hardship, surviving on a simple meal of sadza each day, yet they greeted us with smiles when we visited. A day was spent conversing, singing, playing, dancing and distributing fruits, vegetables and eggs for the coming days. There is something about the African gene when it comes to dancing—and these little angels surely had the moves! It was pure joy to watch them. However, we were also aware that the next time we visited, a child or two would have passed away from HIV. Life was short for most Zimbabweans, as the AIDS epidemic spread throughout the country. Fields were soon filled with graveyards as far as the eye could see. There came a time when coffins became scarce due to lack of timber and rising costs. The nuns would request us to provide blankets to wrap and bury the dead. We complied as much as we could.

Towards the end of each year, we held the DSA Ball, which was a formal sit-down dinner for three hundred people, at a five-star hotel. All the embassies provided their support along with many private companies, airlines, restaurant owners, well-to-do businesses and generous local elites. Food, drinks and desserts for the grand evening were contributed by all embassies, each showcasing its own national cuisine and cultural grandeur. It was a themed event that was eagerly awaited, with tickets sold to raise money for charity. The evening included entertainment by local musicians, a lottery and dancing. Although it was hard work, it was worth it, with everyone coming together for a humane cause. The proceeds were utilised to help women become self-reliant. With the help of Air India and Kenya Airways, I was able to procure a consignment of wheelchairs from India for the disabled, as well as sewing machines, needles, threads, wool, knitting needles, fabrics, blankets and other commodities.

While we faced many challenges in Zimbabwe, the experience was also spiritually fulfilling in some ways. Today, President Mugabe is no more; a new government and new leaders rule the country, but it seems not much has changed. I can only hope that one day Zimbabweans will live in peace and enjoy a stable future like the three majestic rocks themselves.

Virgin Land and Eighteen Days
Tajikistan

ANURADHA MUTHUKUMAR

It all started with the cancellation of my spouse's assignment to Sri Lanka, after which he was reassigned to a newly established nation where India was to open an embassy. No one had heard of Tajikistan (a republic in the erstwhile Soviet Union). My mother's words still ring in my ears, 'Do you ever go to a country that we don't have to search for on a map?'

A tiny country separated by eleven kilometres of no-man's land in what was undivided USSR. That was Tajikistan. The ministry had very little information (almost next to nothing) on the living conditions, culture or customs. Reference books waxed eloquent about Uzbekistan but Tajikistan may well have not existed, but for a few lines about the famous Dushanbe Bozor (Monday Bazaar). Even *Encyclopaedia Britannica* had nothing more than a short write-up, no longer than half a page.

A scrutiny of facts and figures from every source possible laid bare one important fact: winters were going to be exceptionally cold. Members of the mission who were already there said that the central heating system in most homes had either broken down or lacked the fuel or energy to keep them going. Civil war had devastated the economy, rendering repair or maintenance of utility services near impossible. There was almost no public transport. The one saving grace was that there was plenty of running water. However, the pipes were old and rusted; the water that gushed out was a strong flow of reddish-brown liquid. This water had to be filled in containers, left unused until all the sediments settled, filtered again and again, boiled and filtered one last time before it finally became usable and potable. That having been resolved, how was one going to deal with the long harsh winter without the luxury of central heating? Wood was in short supply. The fireplace could offer no comfort. It looked like it was going to be endless days huddled around a sigri, or like the Kashmiris, we could walk around with a kangri under a phiran. After many discussions with experts, amateurs and professionals, my mother's elder sister came up with the most workable solution. She recollected that in her childhood days, goat and sheep droppings which had been formed into balls and dried were used for the sigri that heated the rooms. It was cheaper and far more combustible than cow dung cakes, which were used in the kitchen chulah. What a story that would have made for any grand nieces and nephews: foraging for goat and sheep droppings, shaping and drying them to keep the hearth and home warm! Alas, any possibilities of such tales and other grandmother stories died a natural death; much after the assignment had been signed, sealed and announced, we were casually informed by a colleague that it was a non-family posting. This meant that I had to stay back in Delhi while Mr Ambassador Extraordinary and Plenipotentiary set out alone on a journey to virgin lands waiting to be discovered.

Be that as it may, there was nothing stopping determined little me from venturing out on my own and at my own expense. Thence began eighteen days of pure excitement and adventure that made for unforgettable and everlasting memories. The very first adventure was flying over a neighbouring land where the people, customs and eating habits are more or less like our own. The flight path the aircraft took was over rural Pakistan. From way up there, you saw huge landholdings where the ownership seemed to rest with one single zamindar family. The entire panorama was dotted with small mud houses with only one large pucca villa. This was confirmed by the passenger sitting next to me, a widely travelled and adventurous businessman who also happened to be one of the owners of the airline. He enlightened me on the existing feudal framework.

There was a mandatory halt at Lahore. Documents had to be verified to ensure that the airline was carrying valid and updated papers and permissions. This appeared to be an 'aha moment' as well as an unexpected opportunity. My father was born there, and I was hoping to be able to set my feet on the ground, even if for a few minutes. No such luck! A host of severe-looking men in uniform entered the aircraft, giving us instructions to remain seated. Once they had completed their scrutiny, they returned to the tarmac, but remained on vigil. Anyone who wished to catch a whiff of fresh air was allowed to come to the door and the landing step but no further.

The onward journey took us over Afghan terrain. Scary to behold because all that met the eye were miles and miles of seemingly barren mountains with no habitation in sight, not even a mule trail. My hyperactive imagination went into 'what if' mode: what if the plane crashes? What if there is engine trouble? What if ... what if ... The tragic heroine in me was recalling all the movies about air crashes and the travails of the few who miraculously survived, while others perished on the way or managed to make their way back to some kind of inhabited settlement. Thankfully, there was no mishap and we landed in Dushanbe, the capital of Tajikistan. The airport brought back childhood memories of landing in Kathmandu: the same small, single-storeyed terminal, low hills all around, lush with vegetation and clean, crisp air. It was nearing 5.30 p.m. The sun was setting when, lo and behold, birds of every size and hue took to the sky, flying in murmuration in circles! A few minutes later, they were gone, leaving everything enveloped in the fading twilight.

Remembering this idyllic scene always brings to the fore another memory of landing in another place, equally beautiful and scenic, but encounters that were quite the opposite. On our way to 'a bend in the river' Kinshasa, the capital of then Zaire, now the Democratic Republic of Congo, there was an aircraft refuelling halt at Goma. Our knowledge of French was limited to a few words and a phrase or two; beyond 'Madam et Monsieur' we didn't understand a single word of the announcement. Seeing that we weren't making an effort to deboard, the airhostess informed us that we had to join the others in the terminal building. Thinking that it wouldn't take very long, we left our hand luggage and rose to join the others. Once we got off the plane, I asked a fellow traveller how long the halt would be. According to him, it could be fifteen minutes or fifteen hours, depending on how luck was going to favour us. Alarm bells started ringing in our hearts and minds. Our precious twelve-string guitar had also been left behind on our assigned seat. However, the same gentleman reassured us with an amused grin that it would be safe, as it certainly wasn't covered in gold or studded with diamonds. Good karma and lady luck were on our side; in another thirty minutes we were asked to board the aircraft again. Much to our surprise, it was as if a starter's gun had been fired. Everyone picked up their bags and charged ahead. Our newly found acquaintance came to our rescue once again, asking us to hurry if we wanted to get a seat. It was now a matter of first come, first served, as more passengers were boarding the flight from here. Should the flight be overbooked, we might even find ourselves standing in the aisle! I still wonder if he was pulling our leg and enjoying a soft chuckle at our expense. If he has an elephant's memory, he might still be enjoying an occasional chuckle. Our seats were still reserved for us and remained unoccupied. The next shocker was awaiting us at the arrival hall in Kinshasa. A melee of pushy, boisterous but friendly Zairians, along with people speaking a cacophony of French, Lingala and broken English, came at us from every direction. They were keen to be the first to get our attention, all in good faith, offering assistance and a speedy exit through airport formalities and a ride into town. We were blessed that colleagues from the embassy had received the telex announcing our arrival.

Having reminisced and veered off track, I should get back to Dushanbe. They said I had brought festive cheer when I arrived: It was the first time that any international organisation was holding a gala event for the 'who's who' and others 'who were not'. The office of the United Nations Development Programme was celebrating twenty-five years of the United Nations. As we approached the diplomatic circle, my husband pointed to the tallest and most distinguished-looking person among them as the Iranian Ambassador, and explicitly instructed me not to shake hands with him. According to Iranian custom, a woman shaking the hand of an unknown man was an absolute no-no. A graceful namaste led to a few moments spent with a friendly, warm and welcoming gentleman. The formal ceremony was followed by dinner, a mostly Tajik fare of baked samosa (which they call sambosa), grilled lamb laden with fat, a refreshing, thick yoghurt-based cheesy dip for the lavash and naan, Tajik Plov and big, juicy seasonal fruit, the likes of which I'd never seen before. Melons have never been a favourite, and preferably avoidable, but these were to die for: peachy rich in colour, juicy, aromatic and yet not cloyingly sweet. The grapes were almost the size of prunes with just a hint of tarty flavour that gave the sweet juicy fruit a special taste.

By a quirky twist of fate, my arrival, too, was much celebrated as the first diplomatic spouse to venture a visit to this quaint yet civil war–torn country. It was quite embarrassing to arrive at the UN event to find oneself the cynosure of all eyes. Let's put it down to the sight of a real-life Indian lady in a bright Kanchipuram sari. This was a first for many Tajiks, who until now had only a celluloid experience of Bombay cinema. Yours truly, however, did not fit the bill. All Indian women were supposed to be ravishing dusky beauties with long and lustrous flower-bedecked hair.

Tajiks are avid Indian cinema watchers and love to sing the songs without knowing a word of Hindi. Listen carefully and while you may find the words gibberish at times, the rendition is near perfect. Many dream of going to Bombay to see their favourite movie stars. Somewhere in our junk—which we called treasure—is a newspaper cutout of the Tajik president and his twelve-year-old son meeting Amitabh Bachchan in Bombay.

After the noise and pollution of Delhi, night-time in Dushanbe was a delight. The night sky was spectacular: an inky star-filled sky seemingly close enough to touch. A scarcity of fuel and the uncertainty of war resulted in pin-drop silence, but for a few barking dogs, intermittent family quarrels and an occasional exchange of gunfire in the distance. Sounds travelled loud and far, giving the impression it was next door.

The serenity of the night before was the harbinger of a rude awakening to reality the next morning. A bomb exploded right across from the hotel we were staying at, in a park which, in the darkness, I mistook for a forest! Mayhem and confusion ensued, but fortunately no one was harmed. I wonder who it was meant for, as the only ones in the park at that early hour were the cleaning ladies.

Historically, the word 'Dushanbe' was mentioned during the Kushan era; etymologically, it is derived from the Persian 'Du', meaning 'two', and 'Shanbe' meaning 'Saturday'. Put together, it means the second day following Saturday, that is, Monday. The capital of Tajikistan was built on the site of a centuries-old famous trade point on the Silk Route, where a weekly Monday bazaar was held. Modernisation and development may have changed things today, but back then the bazaar was still the high point of the week, ever more so in a war-ravaged young nation where scarcity was the name of the day. A must-do event on our bucket list. This marketplace was mind-boggling, even for an Indian experienced with weekly street bazaars. Long rows of people plonked on the ground, no stalls, no pushcarts, just a bit of tarpaulin on which they spread out their worldly goods: a needle, lengths of thread, odd mismatched pieces of crockery, cutlery, family heirlooms—anything and everything that could earn a Somoni or two. We were a group of seekers of excitement, experience and rudimentary essentials such as cutlery, crockery and pots. Everyone, except yours truly, was on assignments that would last longer than a few days. Sadly, while entering the country, we could only bring a suitcase of clothes, toiletries and a few sundry necessities. The whoops of glee and hurrahs every time someone found just what they wanted or needed, even if it was just a fork or a knife that matched the spoon they had found at the bazaar the previous week, cannot be imagined. I had come for the experience and a chance discovery of anything unusual or quaint. My trophy was a Russian square shawl which I carried draped over my arm for want of a carry bag. It's amazing how many times I was stopped and asked if it was for sale.

During summer, the country is awash with plenty of fruits, dry fruits and vegetables of the best quality, all naturally grown sans chemical pesticides or fertilisers. There is an abundance of pistachios, although rather small in size, almost half the size of the imported ones available in the Indian market today. You could buy them from the little boys who hung around the hotel. The unshelled pistachios were strung into garlands, as were the unshelled apricot seeds, and had been boiled in salt water. The salty, nutty flavour was a treat to the senses and became a favourite snack, making me one of their cherished customers who always had a load of toffees in both pockets. They should have been in school, but most of the teachers were away, working at other jobs to augment their meagre salaries, which often came months later. Yet there were some diligent people like the professor at the university who took up the position of a cook with the Ambassador and came to his residence after conducting classes. He made for excellent company, but incidentally he knew little about cooking, yet was an eager and fast learner.

Tajiks are warm, friendly and hospitable people. A guest is to be honoured with the best, even if it means sharing their last piece of naan (pronounced nawn, rhyming with lawn) or requesting the neighbours for anything they might have. An officer who was with the United Nations Peacekeeping force recalled instances where he and his colleagues were always welcomed with warm greetings and an invitation to share a meal, regardless of whether there was enough for themselves. This was truly 'breaking bread together', bonding over food and forging relationships.

Tajikistan has an ethnically mixed population. They are of Iranian descent, transformed by Arab invasions and Turkic invaders, part of the Mongol empire and Russian conquest. The women are beautiful and the men handsome, with features, colouring and build that reflect varied ethnicities. A phenomenon that seems unusual is how siblings born of the same parents could be so different, not in character or nature but in physical appearance. One may resemble someone of Iranian and Central Asian descent, with lustrous dark hair and expressive dark eyes, while the other may be unmistakably Russian, with blond hair, dreamy blue eyes and delicate, fine skin.

With relatively few places to go to in the evenings, the one destination was Thank God, It's Friday, the open house venue for expatriates, visiting officials and the like. It was the ideal place for connecting, networking, gathering information and, most of all, relaxing, especially for those whose work took them in all directions across the countryside. Among the interesting people I met there was a gentleman of German-American descent who lived in the United Kingdom, spoke fluent Japanese and was a direct descendant of the composer Felix Mendelssohn. Despite the uber background that he came from, he had insisted on calling me 'Your Highness'. He is sadly no more, although I do have fond memories of our witty and humorous conversations, just as I have unforgettable memories of a virgin country, yet unspoiled by the vagaries of development and modernisation.

The civil war was escalating and we were told that the next flight out might be the last one for a very long time. All those who were there on short visits or assignments were advised to board and leave, lest they are stuck there forever. I, being one of them, was hastily bundled up and sent packing, back to the noisy, crowded and pollution-filled streets of Delhi. The one saving grace was that I had a job I enjoyed, and friends and family eager to hear my tales of unfamiliar lands and accounts of each day of the eighteen spent there.

Diplomacy by Other Means

Baghdad

SHREEDEVI NAIR PAL

Diplomacy is a peripatetic vocation, both for the diplomat and the family, and our lives are tempered by two constants: We represent India wherever we go and we cannot allow ourselves to ever feel that we have a permanent residence in any place regardless of where we are, at least until retirement. These two facts colour our postings and rightly so. However short the posting, we hit the ground running and waste no time in organising our homes and lives to welcome people from the host country and give them an 'India experience' in the best way we can.

And what good can that do in the larger scheme of things, you may well ask. Not to overstate the case, I believe the spouse's role is to ease the way for the diplomat to work in an environment that is conducive to the building of trust between the host country and the diplomat to achieve common goals and take that relationship forward.

Many of us did this with glad grace, but I felt that the ministry did not appreciate or understand us, and took our work for granted. In the 1970s, the fact that you got to travel and live abroad, when most of your fellow countrymen could not, was considered a great privilege. This was supposed to make up for the lack of a career. Who could explain that for every 'A' posting we had, there were twice as many postings to unfamiliar places where living conditions were deplorable, where even the basic necessities could not be taken for granted, and where we had to be very careful with our words to avoid trouble? We lived, learnt and then some.

Wives of diplomat husbands were discouraged from taking up a job outside the home, so our default career setting would read housewife. Then when you returned to India, you discovered that no job awaited you after a hiatus of a few years. House work was apparently not work. By the time there was a relaxation of this law (Was it ever a law or just the mindset of very orthodox men in positions of power?), many of us were already too old to get back to our former careers in India. On the rare occasions that the wife was granted permission by the head of mission and the ministry to work, the husband's foreign allowance was cut. Slowly, and very gradually, this injunction was relaxed, but it came way too late for many of us. So it should come as no surprise that many of us felt the work of IFS wives was unsung and misunderstood, but that does not mean that there were no highs, no joys or fun times.

When I say that we were much more than appendages to our husbands, I do so from experience. Any account of our lives should reflect our desires and values, our interests and talents, and most of all, our contribution to Indian diplomacy even while they were circumscribed by the rules that defined the role of diplomatic spouses.

Life has never been all glamour even in the most glamorous of postings. Settling into a new country, a new house, finding ingredients for typical Indian meals, these were always challenges.

The image of us women whiling away our time playing bridge in the mornings and dressing up every evening for national day receptions and formal diplomatic dinners is as clichéd as it gets. I would have thought that only the ignorant would have this view, but I encountered this everywhere, both in India and abroad. Very few had any idea of how much work was involved in successfully pulling off such events. For example, I remember at one posting, the Head of the Chancery came to me and said that the allowances for our national day reception would not cover professional caterers, so could I help? There we were, my cook and I, making monstrous amounts of kebabs, chicken tikkas and samosas for about five hundred people. Of course, our work was never compensated. In Botswana, I don't know what I would have done without the other embassy spouses pitching in because there were no Indian restaurants or caterers in Gaborone then.

Everything had to be planned and organised, and as much as I like a challenge, sometimes it could all get too overwhelming. In Jeddah, my cook and I reconstituted Dutch powdered milk (fresh milk was just not available), then curdled that milk to make paneer in order to make six hundred rasagollas for the Indian school function. Only to bin the leftover rasagollas because they had turned rancid and smelly in the heat. I could not bear to look at a rasagolla, let alone eat one, for the next ten years. Mine is not an unusual case. Every foreign service spouse can relate such stories.

We women, unlike our spouses, got to meet the ordinary people of a country because we handled the nitty-gritty of organising the home. In that process, we interacted with school teachers, our children's friends and their parents, as well as the carpenter, the plumber, the electrician, the butcher, the baker—people from all rungs of life in every country we stayed in. And while the embassies were always supportive, there were a lot of things we had to do for ourselves to set up home. Practical everyday matters that were solved by practical everyday people.

Our husbands, on the other hand, mainly interacted with the social and political elite of the country they were posted in. And regardless of where they were posted, they never really had to step out of their comfort zone, as their work environment was more or less the same.

As spouses, we never knew quite what to expect in each posting and relied on those who had arrived before us to show us the way around the many challenges of setting up home in an unfamiliar place. But this also taught my husband and me to make light of our little problems and to find humour in many situations. For example, I gave my husband a beautifully wrapped gift on his birthday, and I will never forget the look on his face and the laughter that followed when he opened his gift. It was a hammer; the only thing available at Orosdibaag, the government shop in Baghdad then. Suffice to say that it is still in use.

I choose to write about our first posting, Baghdad, because it is here that I learnt the ropes of my trade, managed to face adversities, and most importantly, understood the value of friendships with other women, both in the embassy and outside. I can say with absolute conviction that after this posting I was not easily fazed by anything that the powers that be and a difficult posting flung at me. Now let's go to where my journey began: the fabled city of Baghdad. Baghdad was 'the posting that set the course'. The year was 1975. The first posting abroad for my baby and me. My husband, a young probationary officer, was posted to Baghdad as Third Secretary and had preceded us there by three months.

My passage to Baghdad was not propitious, to say the very least. When we landed in Kuwait for a layover, Kuwaiti airport authorities demanded my luggage keys, even though I was carrying a diplomatic passport. My son's silver brush and comb—gifts from my family—went missing from the suitcase. In addition, Air India had simply not bothered to book a room for us at their airport hotel despite the overnight stopover, so we spent the whole night in the uncomfortable bucket chairs of Kuwait Airport.

A day after we reached Baghdad, still sore from sitting all night in plastic bucket seats, my cook and I ventured out in search of basic pantry items. I realised very soon that foraging for food was going to be my primary task during that posting. The first word of bazaar Arabic I learnt was *maaku*, which meant 'I don't have it' or 'not available'. What was its opposite? I never did find out because nothing was plentiful or available.

The lift van that contained all our worldly goods, including all my spices, was really taking its time getting to Baghdad. In the meantime, we were all tired of eating chicken cooked with just salt, tomato paste and some yoghurt masquerading as curry. So imagine my joy when I discovered a wizened old crone sitting with a small platter of whole garam masalas in a nearly empty field serving as a market. She could have stepped straight out of the pages of Shakespeare's *Macbeth*—a long, tattooed chin; a few discoloured teeth; a thin, hooked nose; her body covered in a voluminous black *abaya*. I haggled her down to prices I could afford. And how did we get that chicken for our ersatz curry? Well, that's another story.

I cooked, too, in a manner of speaking. My calamitous first dinner for which I had thrown together twenty cups of rice for twenty people in twenty cups of water and pushed the entire mess into the oven—you can imagine what a disaster that was!—made me realise soon enough that there was more to food than the eating of it. What amazed me was the fabulous food that everyone else, barring me, cooked. I was a mere rookie in this art. I suppose cooking was a challenge when so little food was available in the market. Also, there was little else to do. I realised that, despite the lack of ingredients, I had the time to improve my culinary skills, which I eventually did with the help of the other ladies in the embassy.

What I discovered over a few days was that you really needed to know when essential food items like meat, sugar, milk powder, salt, rice, flour, etc., hit the market. And then chase down the object of desire. I bribed a local butcher with a bottle of whisky every other month, so he would call me when he received a fresh supply of New Zealand lamb. Ditto, the grocery shop owner who got consignments of powdered milk and little cartons of fresh cream. Much later, I discovered that army officers sent from India to train Iraqi officers never had any problem getting anything they wanted, because the all-powerful Iraqi army was keeping most of the food to feed itself.

But desperate times required even more desperate measures. The Indian Embassy would regularly send a *note verbale* to the Iraqi foreign office requesting crates of chicken, eggs, fish (pomfret from Bombay, no less!) and rice. An Iraqi friend of mine, Ibtehal, whose daughter, Dahlia, was the same age as my son, Pasha, came home one day and her eyes nearly popped out when she saw me feeding a boiled egg to my son. She had not seen an egg in three years! So occasionally, I would sneak a few eggs from my portion to her.

But official interventions still did not take care of other everyday needs. Sanitary napkins, vegetables, onions, garlic, ginger, all had been '*maaku*-ed' out of the market. During our two-year stint, I never once clapped eyes on ginger and garlic; green chillies were well beyond our reach; and as for onions, they appeared in the market only once. My husband, our cook Subodh and I rushed out and stocked up on them for the rest of our stay.

For other basic necessities, I depended on those in the embassy who were affluent enough to go to Kuwait regularly.

In the absence of good food, I drooled over the recipe books given by my husband, family and friends, but could not find the necessary ingredients for most recipes. However, I did manage to cull a bread recipe from one of them. The Iraqis ate *sammoon,* a fluffy flat bread similar to naan, made from yeast and flour, which were the only food items found ubiquitously. But we needed our double roti. Over time, I began baking fairly decent bread, though in a kadhai, as there were no loaf tins to be had. I also learnt to blanch and freeze fresh vegetables that were cheap when in season, so that they lasted through a sparse, harsh winter when there was thin frost on the ground and just carrots and spinach in the market, if we were so lucky.

The exception was Marguerite Patten's *Cookery in Colour* which my brother gave my husband on our first anniversary with the message 'Given to Satya because Shree will never learn to cook' on the flyleaf. It was written for post-War Britain and was careful, even parsimonious, with ingredients. Nothing extravagant or expensive, so it played a large part in my culinary experiments there. I remember baking a savoury potato cake and a chicken liver pâté from it, which I spiked with a few Indian spices.

But it was Robert Carrier's *Great Dishes of the World,* a fat, squat book, that brought out the romance of fine dining, and in my case, wishful thinking. I could while away many evenings reading about how he cooked on the film sets of *Cleopatra* or how to make the perfect Chicken Marengo, which he assures us Napoleon's chef invented to celebrate his victory in the Battle of Marengo!

Under the not-so-benign gaze of the Ba'ath Party, the locals kept their mouths shut and their persons entirely to themselves. They were terrified of meeting foreigners, even foreign diplomats from friendly countries like India. All except Ibtehal, who met me openly. She taught English at a local school and even though her English was not very good, communicating with her was way easier than with others. I have often puzzled over the fact that if she could be friends with me, why could the other Iraqis not be friendly as well? I figured it must have had something to do with the fact that her husband was the director of their National Museum and must have been close to the powers that be, perhaps even a member of the Ba'ath Party. But once we left, we never clapped eyes on her or her daughter again. After the bombing of Baghdad, I have often wondered about her and Dahlia's whereabouts. Are they alive? I will never know ... And now I cannot find them because Iraq has gone through so many upheavals, no family is where it was nearly fifty years ago. I also wonder, though not to my credit, whether Ibtehal was allowed to be close to me to keep tabs on me. Not that it really mattered, since both of us were young mothers who shared our experiences as new parents and I learnt my way around Baghdad through her.

A Turkoman lady of uncertain age who lived next door once requested that she come over to practise her spoken English. I propped a ladder against my side of the garden wall so she could climb down into my garden without being noticed. She scurried into the house with a satchel containing Iraqi amber rice perfumed with dill and melt-in-the-mouth broad beans and an English translation of the Quran. I have never forgotten her kindness.

In the bitter cold of an Iraqi winter, we used enormous petroleum heaters on which we kept kettles of boiling water to heat and hydrate the rooms. They were a fire hazard, especially with a small child around, but we had no choice. The house we lived in was sparsely furnished—a bed, a few rickety chairs and a dining table made out of wooden crates—but we survived. The embassy agreed to have a carpenter next door create some furniture items for me, as they were way cheaper than anything you could find in the markets. I remember sitting in his shop, my little son at my knee, watching his deft hands working on my order, both of us quiet, because I didn't speak Arabic, and he didn't speak English. One day, he gave a bunch of seeds to our gardener, muttering something in Arabic that I did not understand. But come summer, the garden below my bedroom window was ablaze with a thousand different coloured zinnias. After the dull colours of winter, what a welcome surprise!

Summer transformed Baghdad. Ibtehal invited me for tea in her garden and I was gobsmacked by what I saw. The green of the grass was studded with hundreds of tiny flowers in shades of blue, yellow, red, pink, purple, white. It was as if a rainbow had come to rest in that little corner of heaven. She told me that one year the Tigris River had flooded the entire neighbourhood and ever since then, come spring, they enjoyed two weeks of this wonderful visual treat. In all our later postings, I have never come across anything quite so beautiful.

In summer, the almond trees were in bloom and white orange blossoms filled the air with their fragrance. The first house we lived in had an orange grove in front and we got buckets of bitter oranges that I did not know what to do with, so I sent them to my neighbours. Some sent me bottles of marmalade made from them, leaving them on the front porch. I never got to know who had made them.

We had very little, could afford very little, yet we were happy. I was delighted beyond words when my husband bought me a sewing machine from the government shop for my birthday. I was equally delighted when I found two small fine china tea bowls with a street vendor. And the five cartons of books on art and poetry that we brought with us, augmented with books from the library at the embassy, were great companions through the most difficult of times. I was also lucky that my husband and I had the time to discuss what we read.

Also, there were friends I made who generously gave of their time and talent. I don't think I can ever forget the friend who saved the day for me at a dinner I was hosting, or a Goan friend who invited us for lunch on the very day we were leaving and fed us our favourite Goan sardine curry and rice, which I cook to this day. A much older colleague of my husband, Mr D.B. Mallik, took both of us under his wing and guided us through the complicated terrain of diplomatic entertaining. He was always the first one to taste my experiments in cooking. I also remember the Ambassador who was kind enough to give me a most extravagantly complimentary confidential report, which he kindly sent to me before dispatching it to the ministry. Yes, in those early days, the wives were also evaluated by Ambassadors. Looking back, I think, what cheek! Especially since we did not get paid for all that we did for our husbands and our country.

We went on to wonderful places where I could do far more interesting things like visiting museums and libraries, even study, but sometimes life teaches you the best lessons. And in that laid-back, quiet place where the people were friendly, if distant, I learnt to watch for changes in nature's cycles, appreciate the simple things that made up my life, bide my turn and ruminate on the interests I might pursue if given the chance. I noticed both big and small things, such as when the huge tree at the edge of the garden, after being bare all winter, suddenly sprouted leaves in different shades of green, so beautiful that I could not stop myself from painting it. And small things like the way the light danced on my little son's hair as he tried to pull out weeds in the brown grass that had died in the harsh winter. Things that in a big bustling city would probably go unnoticed.

Now when I hark back to my time in Baghdad, I do not remember the difficulties as much as the lessons in survival that I imbibed and the warmth and many kindnesses of other embassy wives and locals that made a difficult posting infinitely more bearable. Baghdad taught me to take adversities on the chin, stand my ground, develop interests other than those required of an IFS wife, and most importantly, appreciate the beauty of simple everyday moments.

You've Come a Long Way, Baby!
Austria

ASIYA HAMID RAO

In 1983, when we got posted to Vienna, it was the first time that my husband and I were stepping out of the country. For me, it was indeed a big deal. Barely twenty years old, I had stars in my eyes and a song in my heart—so many dreams, hopes and expectations. What's more, I was going to Europe, the land of glitz and glamour, of music, plays, travel and fun. A la la land, no doubt! In that enchanting world within a world, mine was going to be even more magical than any I could imagine, for I was about to step into the glorious world of the Indian Foreign Service—a world of myriad images, a life of travel to distant and fascinating lands to not only see but also experience the pulse of different countries, a life where different cultures, languages and races converged at dinner tables in elegant homes, at ladies' coffee mornings, at the annual bazaars and various other extravaganzas.

I must say I was sufficiently impressed by all I saw in Vienna: the elegant ivy-covered villas as well as residential blocks with wrought-iron gates. The impressive architecture of the imposing buildings, the opera house, Karlskirche, Votivkirche, Rathaus, St. Stephen's Cathedral, Belvedere, Schönbrunn, Hofburg, the parliament, the museums, all represented various architectural designs and periods—Baroque, Gothic, Art Nouveau and others. I thoroughly enjoyed admiring their exteriors and interiors, but at that time of youthful giddiness what thrilled me most was Prater amusement park with its numerous rides; the scarier and wilder, the better! The city parks were well manicured, the shops enticing. And everything was so spick and span: the shining door knobs and bathroom taps could have vied with the kitchen utensils; the sparkling chandeliers in drawing rooms threw up a million stars; even the people seemed to have just emerged after a facial at a beauty salon. Everything and everyone had the look that I had so far seen only in glossy magazines. There was no dust, no flies and no dirt.

Those were the days when we were far from economic liberalisation and globalisation. My eyes popped out to see the shops flooded with products that all youngsters in India desired. One of the first things I did in those early days was to proudly buy myself a pair of dark blue Levi's jeans. Only those of us who've had to live the first twenty years of life without a genuine pair can understand my thrill at this much-coveted purchase. I also remember that for quite a while I lived on a staple diet of Coke, Mars bars, chips and cookies, or else I thrived on a variety of cheeses on different breads. Not so my better half. In a country famous for its boulangeries, croissanteries and bäckerei, he refused to touch their delectable fare and demanded missi roti for breakfast every day, and there was no way I could have charmed him out of this. The reality of being married and running my own home dawned on me, and with it the realisation that living abroad is not all hunky-dory. Had I been in India, I would have without a doubt left the honours in the hands of a capable cook, but in this far-off land I had no choice but to learn to hold the rolling pin. One had the choice of taking one or two domestic helpers on postings abroad, depending on one's seniority; we preferred not to, as we thought managing a household of two wouldn't be hard with a bit of help from a weekly maid. So, every morning I'd wake up to the cheerful music on Radio Danube and while sipping a mug of tea (the long leaf Darjeeling tea transported from home), I'd be ready to roll out missi rotis in all shapes and sizes. Undoubtedly, in my naiveté, I must have believed the myth that the way to a man's heart is through the stomach. Subsequent generations of women were so much smarter and understood well that this is an elusive idea, a yarn spun to extract top-notch culinary service free of cost. They are also lucky to now have umpteen order-ins at their disposal. It is such a pleasure to see that these days the kitchen is, at least sometimes, the domain of both men and women. And how wonderful to see that the world is beginning to understand that a woman, too, has a heart that might need 'reaching'.

I decided to throw myself into the onerous task of learning to cook with wholehearted enthusiasm. But I made a blunder. I started from Z to A, instead of the other way around. Among the first dishes I tried were gulab jamuns and cake. Needless to say, the result was disastrous: the gulab jamuns turned out rather like cannonballs and the cake could have tested the strongest of teeth! The two nearly broke the bin in my attempt to trash them out of sight! I felt quite dejected at these failed attempts. But, as they say, every dark cloud has a silver lining. Mine was in the form of the many well-wishers among senior wives, who took me under their wing and showed me much kindness not only by way of advice but by also giving me time, demonstrating simple cooking (and later, party food too). Gradually, I was able to produce a simple meal of daal, rice, some vegetables and even chapatis. I also learnt to make parathas and, if I may add, even at the expense of sounding boastful, my assortment of parathas soon earned a formidable reputation among the embassy fraternity.

My memories of those days are inextricably linked to the many instances of large-heartedness and generosity shown to me by the Ambassadors' wives—first, Mrs S.K. Singh, and later, Mrs Hiremath. The former initiated me into the world of formal dinners with all the trappings of an elegant table, good food and gracious hosting. The latter did everything a mother would have done when our elder daughter, Aliya, was born. Right from fixing the baby's comfortably warm bath and the oil massage preceding it to the burps and changing of nappies, it was Mrs Hiremath who taught me everything. In fact, she brought me straight from the hospital to her house, insisting that we stay for a month or so until I had regained some energy and learnt to handle a newborn. Mrs Menon, Mrs Gopal and Alka were also very caring and gave me valuable guidance and demonstrations in cooking and housekeeping. Throughout my husband's career, I implemented the party tips handed down to me by Mrs Menon:

- Rule 1. Make sure to keep a balance between vegetarian and non-vegetarian dishes.
- Rule 2. Strike a balance between gravy items and dry items.
- Rule 3. For parties, avoid making dishes that require too many last-minute touches.
- Rule 4. Include a cold dish in summer, apart from salad and raita.
- Rule 5. Ensure that the dishes are of different colours: green, yellow, brown, white, multicoloured, etc.
- Rule 6. Never lose sight of people's religious sensitivities; hence, never serve food that is taboo for religious reasons.
- Rule 7. It's a good idea to ask your guests beforehand about any dietary restrictions.

I must say that these tips, along with others that I imbibed from her, turned out to be extremely useful, and whenever I tried to deviate from them, I regretted it later.

During my journey as a foreign service spouse, I observed that a decade or two later, the wives of officers were less naïve and far more independent. Many of them were highly qualified, regardless of whether they chose to work or not. The world, too, had moved ahead quite a bit and various conveniences were now available to them. It had become commonplace to order one or two dishes from Indian restaurants abroad, and sometimes they catered the entire dinner. The table decor and setting had undergone a loosening of formality. So as a hostess, their task has become somewhat less onerous. On the flip side, many of them now carry an emotional burden—that of having to give up a career; or in case they do manage to keep working, most often in the home country, it is no easy task to manoeuvre the two worlds without doing damage to one or the other. I'm not sure if senior wives take the younger ones under their wing any more, or even if there is any need for it, as the young ladies of today are far more mature, confident and capable.

Back in the days of our first posting, Mrs Singh made it a point to invite us to numerous sit-down dinners. She would call me to her house in the morning itself so that I could observe and learn everything that goes into hosting a formal sit-down dinner. Right from the samosas, canapés and vol-au-vents to the flower arrangements, I would watch everything with wide-eyed wonder. It was, however, the actual dinner in the evening that would make me quite a Nervous Nelly. The table in its full length for eighteen persons was a daunting sight, what with all the cutlery, the stem glasses, name cards and the crisp white damask napkins (that I was only too uneasy about soiling with oil and turmeric stains). Even in those days when I was inexperienced, I knew the basic rule of 'outside in', but I was rather unnerved at the sight of all the cutlery and lived in constant fear of making a mistake. The number of glasses would disconcert me even more, and I was mortally afraid of consuming alcohol by mistake and unwittingly breaking my promise to my parents. The variety of food carried on silver trays and dished out of large serving bowls by poised, white-gloved bearers only added to my consternation. Often, the food was unfamiliar to me: asparagus, avocado, broccoli and baby varieties of veggies. These were usually paired with a particular type of sauce, which, at times, resembled a blob of toothpaste sitting pretty in a corner of the plate. It was truly a relief when the ritual of the formal dinner was over. Of course, over the years I learnt to handle such matters with ease.

Conversation at these soirées generally revolved around travel. I was fairly clueless about most of these destinations, at least as an actual experience. I knew Paris, London, New York, Madrid, as well as Vienna, but as small dots in my geography and history textbooks in school. In contrast, those ladies in stilettos and pearl strings (some long and some short, some double and some single) and Cartier brooches had actually been to these cities several times. That was indeed quite a novelty to me. However, references to places in London by the diplomatic circle ladies had a slightly familiar ring, perhaps due to exposure to English literature in our schools and colleges, and perhaps because England was our fathers' favoured destination for higher studies (much less so the mothers of that generation who mostly obtained their BA or MA degrees in humanities from Indian universities). However, I knew very little of Paris, my knowledge being confined to the Eiffel Tower and French perfumes. I knew nothing of the boulevards, quartiers and cafés of this glamorous city. I suppose, since my antennas were very receptive to cultural insights, I was a fast learner. I might venture to say that very soon I was able to pronounce French words with an impeccable accent. *Mais oui! C'est vrais!*

Art was another topic of discussion and often very detailed and informed analyses would follow. I had seen the works of Indian artists in museums and art galleries in Delhi, as well as some Ram Kumars in my grandmother's house, but my exposure to European artists was limited. I recalled my house in Aligarh, where prints of paintings by Degas, Monet and Van Gogh hung on the walls. These had been picked up by my father from the museum shops of Europe during his 'grand tour' after completing his PhD at the University of Manchester in the late 1950s. Several other houses also had prints of the grand masters, with the Mona Lisa being a particular favourite. But that was all. On my arrival in Vienna, in the first fortnight itself I had visited the Kunsthistorisches Museum (Museum of Art History) and the Belvedere with its impressive collection of Klimt, Kokoschka and Schiele, among others. I thoroughly enjoyed these and subsequent visits to other museums; the masterpieces, whether paintings or objets d'art, fascinated me.

Another popular topic of discussion at these soirées was visits to concerts and operas, which were then whetting the cultural appetite of the city. Vienna's erudite afficionados never missed any performance. I gathered that cultural outings like these would be followed by dinner at a Michelin-star restaurant. I had heard of Mozart, Beethoven, Schubert, etc., but hardly knew anything about their music. (And what are these Michelin-star restaurants? I was puzzled!) My father had tried to introduce my siblings and I to Western classical music, but it was a failed attempt. We preferred qawwalis, ghazals and Hindi film songs. In addition, I listened to ABBA, Boney M, The Carpenters, etc. In Vienna I tried to develop some appreciation of Western classical music; even though my knowledge remained very limited, I began to enjoy it, especially live concerts. I cannot say the same for opera, although I gave it a try. I found the extremities of high-pitch and low-pitch sounds not pleasing to the ears. Once during one such effort at developing some taste for it, I decided to watch the operetta *Die Lustige Witwe* (*The Merry Widow*) on television. Our elder daughter, Aliya, who was then a baby, was cosily ensconced in her bouncer, cooing away merrily, while I started to watch the opera. Soon, I heard uneasy sounds coming from her direction. I noticed her face contorting with strange expressions, as though she was in great pain. This was followed by inconsolable hollering. I panicked, thinking something grievous had happened to her. Leaping to my feet, I hurriedly took her out of the bouncer to examine her carefully after switching off the TV. Immediately, the crying subsided into a whimper and then stopped entirely. Phew!

Since I was such an 'Alice in Wonderland', I would mostly stay quiet during these discussions, while picking up titbits to better equip myself socially. Slowly and gradually, I found myself more confident and fairly at ease. Over the decades, I found that being the spouse of a diplomat is a lifelong learning experience, with many facets to it, ranging from VIP, prime ministerial to presidential visits, cultural weeks and exhibitions to visits of artists, writers, sportspersons and film stars; in all of these, the spouse plays a fairly important role, more so the Ambassador's wife. Often these are cherished memories and the experience leaves one richer. Soon after we reached Vienna, we found the embassy gearing up for the official visit of Prime Minister Indira Gandhi. Her daughter-in-law, Sonia Gandhi, and the grandchildren, Priyanka and Rahul, were to accompany her. I was given the duty of accompanying the grandchildren from morning to evening to the sightseeing and other programmes planned for them. In addition, I was to accompany Sonia and the two children to an opera one evening. I was delighted, and those three days turned out to be quite a memorable experience for me. I remember the first day when I went to pick up Priyanka and Rahul from their hotel, Sonia instructed me politely to make sure that the children were kept away from prying journalists. Most embassy ladies were involved in some task or the other for this very high-profile visit. The Ambassador's wife, Manju Singh, was in hospital recovering from a fracture, but she supervised matters from there, looking into the minutest of details, such as instructing the hotel staff to put yellow roses in the prime minister's room (Mrs Gandhi's favourite). The visit was a huge success. Everyone was happy with it, as well as with the courtesies shown by the VIP family.

One of my most treasured memories of Vienna was the time when M.F. Husain stayed with us in our modest apartment in Sievering, Vienna's wine-growing district. It was a pleasure and an honour. I was overjoyed at the thought of hosting such a great artist. The very first day, Husain saheb announced without preamble that he wanted to paint my portrait. Imagine my joy! That same evening my husband, our friend Ranjit, Husain saheb and I went for a stroll on Vienna's famed pedestrian zone, Kärntner Strasse. After some time we decided to stop by Sacher's for a cup of coffee and Sacher torte. A little drama followed. Husain saheb, as was his wont, was barefoot, and the doorman to the café wouldn't allow us in, as the café had a fairly strict dress code. My husband and Ranjit tried to persuade the manager, informing him that Mr Husain was no ordinary person. The manager was a stickler for rules and wouldn't budge. Finally, Ranjit had to call the office of the Austrian chief of protocol and the matter was sorted out.

It must be said that not all special experiences are pleasant. At times, VIPs can be demanding, fussy and impolite. There are also other kinds of experiences that can be harsh, like serving in war zones where, at times, there may be loss of life. There are places where availability of common groceries is difficult. Then there are places where one may experience extreme weather conditions. In August 1998, when we reached Dhaka for our posting, we found ourselves in the midst of the worst flood of the century that the country was witnessing. Dhaka's roads had become like canals where boats were being used for transport. Most cars would get stuck in the water, except for the large Range Rover varieties. Sometimes those too would get stuck and then we had to stand in waist-deep slushy water, with water snakes slithering by!

In 2011, when we were posted to Saudi Arabia, it required a different kind of adjustment. Coming from Aligarh, I had seen instances of segregation at private functions like weddings, with separate areas for men and women. I was also familiar with modest dressing and even the observance of hijab and the wearing of abaya by some women. But in Saudi Arabia segregation was practised to an extreme level, and the abaya was 'imposed' on all women, both Saudi nationals as well as foreigners. I believe the situation has changed in the kingdom since then, with some degree of flexibility now being observed.

For many of us in the foreign service fraternity who come from small towns and cities of middle-class India, the transition to diplomatic life is scattered with instances of awkward moments and nervousness. Most of us surmount these challenges and learn to glide smoothly. When I reflect on the first twenty years of my life, I find they were entirely different from life in the foreign service. I grew up in the small university town of Aligarh, where my father was a professor at Aligarh Muslim University. People were simple, and life even simpler. The interiors of houses were modest, as was the lifestyle of the inhabitants; several university staff commuted on bicycles. There, too, we occasionally had dinners at our house and at others', but they were very different from the formal RG (Representational Grant) dinners. The focus was on the food, not much on table decor, except for the special dinner set which would be brought out from the confines of a sideboard and the best table cover. The menu was by and large almost always the same in every house at these daawats, as they were referred to over there: qorma, biryani, shami/seekh kababs; and for vegetarians, who were negligible in number, there was mostly dhuli urad daal or matar paneer. The dessert was almost always phirni or shahi tukda, occasionally fruit cream or trifle. For Eid dinner, there were two types of dessert: qiwami sewain and sheer khurma. Serving alcohol was quite unheard of. The only drinks served were colas and nimbu paani, with peanuts for snacks. There were just a handful of homes where alcohol was served, and I think sometimes my parents had a challenging time refusing it without causing offence to the host and hostess. I remember both my parents lowering their heads slightly and doing their aadaabs at every such offering, with an equally polite refusal, 'Ji nahin, nawaazish ka bahut shukriya' (No, please. Thank you so much for your kindness.).

Sometimes when I ponder on my personal journey, starting from a modest background, I can't help thinking, 'You've come a long way, baby!'

But then I wonder, 'Have I really?'

The Devils Wear Prada

Switzerland

PREETI SINGH

The thirty-odd years spent abroad as a diplomatic spouse were interesting, to say the least. Besides the upheavals created by moves, settling down in different homes, domestic help problems, endless entertainment and numerous schools for our son, every new city in a new country made one's powers of observation go into overdrive. On average, it took about three months to settle down, and thereafter, everything novel was experienced, thought about and discussed.

For me, the greatest reward of a peripatetic life was to note the cultural differences between life in India and the ways of another country. All of the countries we visited as a family either made us vehemently affirm what we believed in or modify our previously held convictions, making us less judgemental about what we saw around us. There were some epiphanies too, especially regarding our Western-oriented education, which had led us to unquestioningly believe in the superiority of Western ways. There were some encounters with insidious racism that made our blood boil before it could cool by understanding the ways of history and its consequences.

The White race would always be the White race, and it was up to us to find ways to come to terms with this fact. After all, we were not tourists on brief holidays but temporary residents who had to function effectively on a daily basis. This was especially true for our school-going children—every three years in an international school brought new classmates and teachers, which, in hindsight, would become a significant part of their formation as human beings. And we parents had to, willy-nilly, respond in meaningful ways to their problems and offer useful advice—or so we hoped.

Our postings in the Arab world and Afghanistan called for a different type of response and adjustment. Their cultural identity and social practices were distinct from what we had experienced so far. In their personal lives, diplomats can live according to their own beliefs and values, without any pressure from the locals to change their stance on any issue. However, there is no stopping anyone from observing different beliefs and the contradictions they may encompass. In English-speaking countries, it is a different story. The English language is a boon, allowing access to the media, literature and popular culture. In Europe, language differences can be a problem. Many Europeans know English to varying degrees, but will choose to speak in their own language, making it clear that if you do not understand it, it is your problem.

Apart from France and Germany, other European countries are quite small, both in size and population. However, whether big or small, the people of each country are very aware of their unique identity and spend ample time emphasising this to temporary residents like us, who have easy access to them because of our diplomatic status. I cannot count the number of lunches and dinners where I have been given detailed explanations of how each group is 'unique' in terms of language, customs and character stereotypes.

For instance, I've often been told that Swiss Germans are different from other Swiss, and this difference makes living in one Swiss city distinct from another. Thus, living in Zürich can be quite different from living in Montreux or Basel, or even Neuchâtel. Considering that the whole of Switzerland has a population of only seven million—about the same as South Delhi, maybe?—I am amazed at how people of a small, highly developed nation can go to such lengths to pinpoint the differences among themselves.

Europeans are also, generally, quite snobbish. If members of a family can trace their roots back to a certain area for three to four generations, they consider themselves quintessential insiders, having the birthright to behave in an uppity way. Of course, such families are also inheritors of small or large fortunes, with a few classy chateaus thrown in for good measure.

Having visited quite a few of these chateaus during our various travels in Europe, I must say they are quite beautiful. Not all are large—this fact quite defied my preconceived notions—but they are very quaint, with beautiful (though somewhat ragged) upholstery, carpets and curtains, ornate gold-framed portraits of ancestors and stylish furniture. Given the overall demographic profile of Europe, the inheritors are generally super-senior citizens, frequently with barely enough cash flow to maintain the premises. In fact, inviting visitors like us to tour them—for a fee—is often one way of generating money to keep them running.

And yet, such genteel poverty does not deter them from having a view on the 'immigrants' in their midst—or even about sari-clad spouses like yours truly. I can recall many daytime gatherings where I was looked at askance: *What is she doing here among us? Why is she asking all these questions?* At least, this is what their eyes seemed to convey, quite forgetting that it was their Diplomatic Wives' Association that had invited me in the first place.

The women of this species can be identified quite easily. They all arrive in old pricey cars, dine in the city's best restaurants and shop in the most expensive stores. They are often, though not always, blonde. And they are slim—one might even say *too* thin—with crow's feet around their eyes and lips, and gnarled hands. They spend a fortune on their heavily coiffured hairdos and wear rather large stone jewellery, shiny patent shoes, red nail polish and, of course, designer clothes. It is the latter that often proves to be their undoing.

I remember one summer's social calendar being fuller than ever, with numerous dinner parties and early evening receptions. It is natural that anyone worth their salt would have a garden full of flowers—especially roses and rose vines—in the prime weeks of a European summer. And if you do, what better way to show it off than to invite the city's who's who—diplomats do get included in this list sometimes—to an evening reception when days are long and the weather balmy, with the above-mentioned vines of roses and other summer flowers wafting their fragrance on the summer air?

The story below is a real experience that took place one gorgeous summer evening in Geneva. My husband and I were the only Indians present, and I was quite prepared for an evening conducted in French, of which I know very little. Not expecting to be part of any meaningful conversation, I spent the evening watching the other guests come and go.

So, I found myself dressed in a light summer sari, walking through our host's fancy living room (with my husband) towards the garden beyond, escorted by a nose-in-the-air maid dressed in a black skirt, white prim blouse, a spotless eyelet apron and shiny black court shoes. She had already sized us up, her lips fixed in an automatic smile but her eyes conveying something else. The hostess saw us and gushed forward, giving me an affectionate hug, kissing me three times on the cheeks in true Swiss style. She did the same with my husband while I walked forward to be subjected to the same by her banker husband. It was all very posh: the house, the maid, the hosts, the garden and the guests. Soon, the titbits came around served in silver trays with the mandatory lace doilies setting off both the silver and the food.

I looked around. We knew some people, but not all. Everyone was talking the way people do at these receptions: wine glass in one hand and titbits in the other, shifting body weight from one foot to the other. They were dressed to the nines—designer clothes, no doubt, and from the finest labels. While I do not wear western outfits myself (other than casual trousers), I have always been interested in clothes and patterns, colours and cuts.

And so my eye caught one of the women wearing what I knew was a Prada outfit, and I immediately recalled where I had first seen it: in the window of the Prada store in Rêve. Yes, there it was, a pista green blanket check skirt and jacket with fringed cuffs. It didn't look very grand, but it was a Prada alright. The wearer was speaking animatedly in rapid French, and the way she cast her eyes around, it was obvious that she knew she was completely 'with it'.

And then ... Mid-sentence, I saw her face change. She stopped talking, a quick grimace crossing her face. I looked around and saw what she had just seen. There she was—another woman, just like her, dressed in a Prada outfit that was EXACTLY the same: a pista green blanket check skirt and jacket with fringe cuffs. And she seemed heading towards her ...

That was enough. The speaker quickly ended her conversation with her interlocutor and began to move away. I looked around.

The newcomer in the similar Prada had also noticed her and had turned away.

That was it—so much money spent on something that someone else of your kind also had. It was enough to make you feel curdled and angry. I'll conclude by telling you there was yet another corollary to this one. As we were leaving, I saw a latecomer enter the garden. She, too, was in a Prada outfit: the same pista green blanket check skirt and jacket with fringe cuffs.

Musings on My First Posting
China

SHARMILA KANTHA

Sometime during our posting in Hong Kong in the early 2000s, I was at a formal dinner talking to an elderly British expatriate. As usual, I was trying to make polite conversation, starting with the ubiquitous introduction line, 'How long have you been here?' But the lady, a slim and elegant person with short white hair, would have none of that and started quizzing me about being a diplomat's wife instead. During the conversation, I shared with her that, fresh out of college, I married a man I had briefly met once before and travelled with him to China in 1983. To my surprise, she appeared aghast at this experience. 'That was some courage on your part!' she blurted out.

This was when I realised, some twenty years after marriage, that what we as Indian girls go through in an arranged marriage is quite astounding. And marriage to a diplomat is doubly so, as we go off to an environment that is completely unfamiliar, where the culture is different, the language unknown and the daily life so unlike what we've known before—all without any family support.

In my case, there was an advantage. My father, Yashwant Sinha, who was then a Director in the Ministry of Commerce (and later became Minister of Finance and External Affairs of India), was posted to the Indian embassy in what was then a capital city, Bonn. Our family was at the time living in the tiny two-room hostel of Curzon Road apartments, and we kids were immensely excited about going overseas. The Germany posting of more than three years remains alive in our memories even today, as it was such an unusual and highly enjoyable period. We loved travelling across Europe, even going on a long camping trip to Scandinavia. We devoured the chocolates, the oats and the bratwurst, and became familiar with the public transport system within a short time, helping visiting Indian guests navigate the city. In six months, after hours of watching local television, we kids had become adept at German. This was important, as in those days the government did not support international school education and we had to move to the local public schools within a few months. We actually ended up doing better than our German classmates in language classes! International student days, Diwali dances, receiving Prime Minister Indira Gandhi during her visit, making lifelong friends and other experiences enamoured me of a diplomatic life.

Since it was a single overseas posting, I probably did not fully grasp what diplomatic life was all about as a child. Once my family had persuaded me that it was time for me to get married, I boldly stated my preference to marry an Indian Foreign Service officer. As luck would have it, Ashok Kantha's parents were scouting around for a bride. Within three weeks, I moved from being a carefree college student to the wife of a Second Secretary. Shortly after my college exams were over, I packed my new suitcases and set off for Beijing.

The first posting is always memorable for a diplomatic spouse, laying the foundations for the next few decades. My recollections of the eighteen months I spent in Beijing are still vivid and I look back on them with great warmth and nostalgia.

The memory that stands out the most from that period is the immense support and affection that I, as a new bride, received from our colleagues in the mission. Ashok had already been there for about two years before coming to India on home leave to get married. Ambassador Venkateswaran and his extremely elegant wife, Usha, were role models we knew we could never fully aspire to be and they were always very approachable. Ashok, who had earlier been posted for language training in Singapore, had his good friend from that posting with us in China as well, along with his wife. They were at the station to receive me when the train from Hong Kong trundled in at six in the morning. I learnt a lot from them about living and coping in Beijing. We had two more postings together and remain close friends. The Counsellor and his wife, Mr and Mrs Puri, had been on previous challenging assignments and took me under their wing as a daughter. Shortly after my arrival, we were joined by a young couple, both of whom were in the foreign service. Another Counsellor, a bachelor, was always ready for an impromptu meal or picnic or any heated debate. He passed away in an accident during his next posting, and we still miss his bonhomie.

All in all, I cherish the friendliness and continuous interactions with the colleagues and staff to this day. It was no big deal to wake up on a Saturday and decide to visit a palace, explore a local market or have lunch or dinner together. The China of those days was an inhospitable land, with road signs that read 'No foreigners beyond this point', where the local shops had nothing much to offer and the few foreigners in Beijing relied on a special shop, the Friendship Store, for their daily supplies. Few cars passed by on the wide roads, which were populated by workers on bicycles, all wearing the same blue jackets and white shirts, looking weather-beaten and dismal.

Fortunately, one of the advantages of living in a communist state was that the government insisted that diplomats hire domestic staff. And so, our household had a cook and an ayi designated by the diplomatic 'services' bureau to do all the cooking, cleaning, shopping and ironing required for the two of us. Every Thursday afternoon, the two of them attended a debriefing session at their office, but as long as we didn't discuss matters of bilateral relations, they were much more helpful than anything else. I learnt most of my Chinese language skills from them, even discussing the intemperate younger generation with the elderly ayi, who was shocked at how couples roamed around in parks 'with their arms around each other'.

I settled in rather quickly, and in retrospect I feel this was because we just did not know any better. I embraced the new life with great enthusiasm and began learning Chinese with a home tutor. Embassy gatherings, diplomatic parties and spouse meetings remained a fixture through our various postings, and I always enjoyed getting to know new acquaintances who quickly became friends.

While I was in Beijing, the embassy ladies ran a primary school in the chancery, which had about eighty children from many countries. As an officer's wife, I was expected to teach there. With no prior experience but with nothing else to do, I enthusiastically took up this new venture, which proved to be disastrous. I was teaching maths to four eight-year-olds in class four, and being a rambunctious and undisciplined lot, they completely destroyed any aspiration I might have had to become a teacher. Many diplomatic spouses have found good careers in international schools at their places of posting, and in hindsight I wish I had been more patient with the kids.

Under the leadership of Mrs Venkateswaran, the teachers undertook interesting initiatives for the students. During my year there, we organised several international days and sports days, which involved months of preparation. I also did a project on Early Peking Man, and Mrs Venkateswaran joined us on a trip to a nearby archaeological site. The kids enjoyed collecting rocks (which may or may not have been tools of Early Peking Man), and the parents appreciated the exhibition we held at the end of the year. All these activities brought us closer and that truly served as the glue that kept us engaged in this strange country.

The language was an issue to begin with. Early on, the lady manning the elevator asked Ashok something in Chinese. Thinking she was asking if I spoke Chinese, I happily responded, 'Not at all!' Turned out she was asking if I missed my parents!

Of course, I missed my parents and family. The only communication with them took place through the weekly mail bag, as telephonic calls remained out of our meagre financial reach. Every Wednesday afternoon, I sat down with long sheets of yellow paper and wrote at least five letters to various members of the family on both sides, each at least three pages long. Since Ashok discouraged me from writing about any woes I might have, I kept the letters cheerful and chatty, detailing our lives of the previous week with great humour. I also kept a diary and wrote several articles for Indian newspapers that actually got published. There was not much news coming from China in those days and my observations about daily life readily found a place in *The Times of India*.

The arrival of the bag was a much-anticipated weekly event. On Friday, the designated person would carry the bag to Hong

Kong, along with a long list of items from many staff members to be purchased there—things like coffee, milk powder or Tang. On Sunday evening, the person would return, carrying newspapers, letters and all the requested supplies. We would enthusiastically greet him at the chancery, eager to pick up our stuff and unwilling to wait until the next day.

My mother, a published author of children's books, wrote faithfully each week, again chatty accounts of what was happening at home. The bag system was not always regular and the first week that I did not receive any letters, I cried my heart out. The next day at school, Mrs Puri gently asked me, 'No letters from home this week?' This made me realise that my emotions were common and understood by everyone. Mail remained a vital part of our lives during our posting in Washington, DC (1989–92), but by the time we reached Kathmandu (1997–2000) and later Hong Kong (2000–03), telephone calls had become much cheaper and letters sadly went out of practice.

By and by, with the help of the home tutor, who came for two hours a week, and due to the necessity of communicating with ayi and the cook as well as people in shops, I picked up Chinese quite well and even studied the characters. It was a great surprise to me that nearly thirty years later, when I returned to China in early 2014 with Ashok, who was then designated Ambassador, the language I dredged up from the recesses of my mind remained intact at that same level. I boldly decided to take the government language capability test, which included reading and writing, and I count as one of the biggest accomplishments of my life the fact that I aced levels four and five. My former teacher, whom I located after thirty years, told me that I was the only diplomatic spouse she had taught who had studied the characters, and she shared with me the letters I had written to her decades ago.

Fortunately, China was the only posting where learning the language was necessary, and that too more a matter of interest, since it was Ashok's designated language and he spoke and read it fluently. In our other postings in Washington, DC, Kathmandu, Hong Kong, Kuala Lumpur and Colombo, most people spoke English. This made our lives much easier. While I never had to cook hundreds of samosas and gulab jamuns for national day receptions in any of our postings, there were two interesting dinners we hosted during our first Beijing posting that really taught me what this important task for diplomatic spouses was all about. One fine summer day, an Indian delegation was travelling from Delhi to Beijing, and my father had sent a box of mangoes with them for us. There was no question of the two of us enjoying the mangoes by ourselves, and we decided to throw a mango party for the embassy officers. Since it was an internal dinner, we asked the cook to keep the food ready and then both he and ayi left for the day. That was my rude introduction to organising a dinner. *Where were the wine glasses? What did we do with the dessert plates?* It took time to take out the dishes and lay them on the table. It also took time to bring out the water glasses and cut the mangoes. By the end of the dinner, the dirty dishes were heaped in the sink and the different glasses—whisky, wine, water and liqueur—were piled up all over the counters. I left the tap leaking that night, and when ayi arrived the next morning, the kitchen was flooded. 'I don't know how this happened,' I mumbled and quickly escaped to the school, leaving her and the cook to deal with the disaster.

This chaotic dinner prepared me well for the next three decades of hosting diplomatic parties. Keep everything ready in advance became my guiding mantra. In Washington, DC—the only posting where I did not have a cook—I borrowed *Bon Appétit* from the local library, browsed my grandmother's ancient cookbook and started preparations a week in advance, including the cleaning, dusting, shopping and, finally, the cooking. In other postings, the cook and I prepared the dishes together, making sure everything was on the table on time and quickly cleared, including four-course sit-down meals.

My other 'learning experience' took place when the sitar maestro Pandit Ravi Shankar was visiting Beijing for some performances. During the rehearsal, he took Ashok aside and said the Chinese food was awful and asked if it would be possible to have some Indian food instead. When I returned from the school that afternoon, I found the cook frantically scurrying around and mumbling to himself, while ayi, usually a laidback soul, was rushing around armed with a broom and a duster. 'Guests, guests!' was the only word I could catch. A few minutes later, Ashok called to inform me that the entire delegation of musicians was coming for dinner and that I would need to provide some Indian food myself, as the cook knew only Chinese and Western dishes. I'm really proud of how I maintained my cool and agreed to the request.

I did have experience with cooking in the sense that I used to bake cakes and pies in the oven my mother had bought in Germany. So I pored over my grandmother's cookbook, which had nice, simple Indian recipes and decided to make potato in yoghurt curry and cucumber raita, among other things. This had to be done quickly because I had to attend Pandit Ravi Shankar's concert that evening, after which everyone would come to our home. Mrs Venkateswaran, who was sitting in the row in front of me, turned around and asked how I was managing at such short notice. I replied quite confidently, as I recall, and she laughed, probably thinking what a duffer I was to be so sanguine despite never having cooked dinner before, especially for such exalted guests!

Of course, the curry and raita were quite a disaster, since the yoghurt turned watery and the dishes ran into each other on the plate. However, the guests were pleased to have even that available instead of Chinese food. I must say that Pandit Ravi Shankar was very friendly and didn't look down at the food, even calling me 'bahu'.

I found all our postings fascinating, offering a wealth of new experiences. Washington, DC had great shopping, and the local library was conveniently located next door. In Hong Kong, the vibrant Indian community regularly organised fabulous parties, including celebrations for Diwali, the Chinese New Year and other occasions. Travelling in Malaysia during our tenure in Kuala Lumpur was a real pleasure. And Sri Lanka, despite the fact that it was recovering from the war, had a beautiful residence where we hosted many delegations and local dignitaries, with the help of catering from Taj Samudra. In Kathmandu, a group of Indian expatriate women, embassy ladies and local aristocracy played bridge regularly.

It was in Kathmandu that we faced a most challenging situation with the hijacking of the Indian Airlines flight. We were at a function when Ashok received a call informing us that the flight had gone missing. From then on, it was a desperate situation. Several embassy members were on that flight, which was held by terrorists in Kandahar for eight nerve-wracking days. One passenger was killed, but after intensive negotiations, the flight was finally released on 31 December 1999. All the officers got together at our place that evening to watch the passengers deplane in Delhi.

The life of a family like ours is unique, with the wife and children all playing roles in the diplomatic community. The diplomat requires immense support and behind-the-scenes assistance, and the family must stand together through thick and thin. Many a time, I have had to advise my son as he grew up overseas to be careful while making friends and to remain mindful that his actions could impact the country's image. Nonetheless, the experiences are like no other, and it is always a proud moment for us to represent our country, even if we have been trudging through the day attending local functions in languages we don't understand, wearing heavy saris and touching up our make-up from time to time. I have accompanied first ladies during their state visits to India, sat through amateurish but enthusiastic community functions, stood for hours in heels to greet nearly a thousand guests at our national day receptions, attended numerous national day receptions of other countries where I smiled inanely at people and helped my son navigate different school systems—International Baccalaureate in one country and US and British in others. I have also gone camping in the US, snorkelled in Malaysia, enjoyed stunning mountain views in Nepal, travelled to remote places in Tibet and Xinjiang, and happily stuffed myself with local dishes everywhere. Through all of this, I have managed to write books and pursue a modest career, thanks to remote working.

There is no other life quite like this.

Ying and Yang
The Korean Peninsula

ANITA SAPRA

Everyone goes on vacations. The excitement and sense of adventure of exploring a new place can be quite intoxicating. What you usually bring back after seeing the sites is a general sense of the country. You definitely miss out on getting to know the people and culture of the region deeply. On the other hand, living in a country for an extended period is truly rewarding; it allows you to get a better understanding of society. As I look back on the thirty years spent in different regions around the world, I find myself transported back to those countries. Whenever I encounter someone or anything associated with them, it reminds me of all the enriching experiences I gained from my time there.

Before I got married, I never imagined that my life would involve globetrotting and moving every three years from place to place. As some of you may already know, according to a survey, moving is the third-most stressful situation after death and divorce.

Being a part of the Indian Foreign Service, my husband took his young bride on his second posting to Saudi Arabia; his first posting had been Egypt. At that time, in 1979, the embassies were located in Jeddah and not the capital, Riyadh. Air India, our national airline, took us to Kuwait, where we were forced to spend the night, as Jeddah airport was flooded due to torrential rainfall. I like what one of the Saudi ministers had said about the outcome of the floods: 'We will be getting a good watermelon crop in the upcoming season.' My kind of person—always looking at the glass half full.

Keeping true to my optimistic heart, I must say there are several positive aspects of being a part of the foreign service family. It helps you bond with spouses of other officers and support staff. We are able to understand each other better and lend support to new arrivals in the mission.

There are many examples of support; the foremost that comes to mind is the Republic Day celebrations in Jeddah in 1980. It was customary for the Ambassador to host a reception in the magnificent front lawns. That year, the weather took a turn, and by the evening it looked like it would rain when the guests were expected. So, with the help of the officers, support staff, security guards and domestic help all the furniture was removed from the spacious reception and dining area. Everyone chipped in to ensure the place was fit to welcome the guests. Finally, after completing this herculean task, when the guests arrived, they were greeted by the officers in their bandhgala coats, lined up and ready. Unaware of the hectic activity just an hour earlier, they were warmly welcomed. Our children also bonded well with other embassy children and their parents. Returning to Delhi, at the External Affairs Hostel, our kids found other children who were facing the same problems as they were. I have overheard my daughters asking other kids if they were also struggling with maths and Hindi, or being teased about their accents by other students. They felt comforted knowing they were not alone. One day, standing in a circle on the lawn, they were taking turns to share where they were from. At that moment, I realised that these kids are our future global citizens. Travelling in itself is an education, and for our family it's been quite an experience. Speaking of learning, in India I had never come in contact with royalty up close. In Madrid, our Ambassador was a maharaja, and during our first dinner at his residence it was strange to hear his helpers addressing him as maharaj.

Every year in January, the king and queen of Spain host the diplomatic corps for a reception at the palace. In 1982, my husband and I were on the guest list. Being a first time for both of us, it felt like being transported back in time as they announced the names of the guests entering the ballroom to meet the royal family. The king, followed by the queen and the two princesses, was there to welcome us. This got me thinking: what would I say if they came over to talk with us later? Dismissing that thought, I reasoned that with so many people, this would never happen. When the royal couple was mingling with the guests, I was very nervous, especially when King Juan Carlos came and stood near me and another diplomat's wife. Luckily, that year the king and queen were to be the chief guests at our Republic Day parade. I very hesitantly asked the king if he had ever witnessed the parade before. Imagine my surprise when he responded that he had seen it and had also captured it on film. He added that if I visited the palace sometime, he would show it to me. I thought to myself: that's never happening! Then he went on to say that this time it would be different, as he would be under the spotlight and, frankly, nervous that he wouldn't even be able to scratch his nose. A valuable lesson was learnt. In my eyes, he was a king, but at the end of the day, he was human just like anyone else, with his own fears and anxieties. In later years, I met royalty from other nations as well, including Saudi Arabia, Kuwait, England, Cambodia and Jordan. Meeting them no longer made me nervous or anxious, and I was able to talk to them like I would with anyone else. The quality that was most prominent among famous people on the world stage, and which impressed me the most, was the humility that many of them possessed. If you ask the people in our service, many will confirm encountering people around the world who love Indian cinema. Imagine attending a reception where the Ambassador from an Arab country asks you about the welfare of Amitabh Bachchan! Or an Egyptian delegation from Cairo Radio singing a Hindi film song on their visit to India. Even in the far-off Caribbean islands, Bollywood music is much loved. Ask any Trinidadian student who comes to learn Hindi at the cultural centre, and they will tell you that the driving force behind it is to understand and sing our religious and film songs. From a diplomatic point of view, it's like preaching to the converted. Two standout incidents showcasing a love for Indian cinema took place in South and North Korea. Yes, my husband is one of the few diplomats in the world who has been posted to both countries. The year was 1988. South Korea was under the microscope, as they were hosting the Olympic Games. I hailed a taxi from our residence to Namdaemun, a market in Seoul. Normally, in India you would tell the taxi driver where you want to go and after that no verbal exchange would take place. No, sir, not in Korea! The taxi driver started asking me questions. I told him I didn't speak Korean. He then started to name countries: Japan, France, Malaysia. I understood he was asking which country I was from. A fair question. I told him, Indo, which is what the Koreans call us. After we got my geographical location out of the way, he happily continued asking me questions in Korean, making me quite nervous, as I had no idea what he was saying. To make matters worse, he kept turning his head around to talk, with just one hand on the steering wheel. The taxi drivers there, I was to learn later, like to chat with their passengers. I was worried he would get us killed in an accident!. When he realised he was not making any progress, he started singing a song from *Haathi Mere Saathi*! He gestured me to sing along. What a rare sight to behold: me in a taxi on the streets of Seoul singing a song in my own language. Later on, I learnt that *Haathi Mere Saathi* was a popular film in Korea in 1975. It was renamed *Holy Elephant*, and many children thronged to watch it in theatres.

The second instance was in 1999 when we were posted to North Korea. The Pyongyang International Film Festival started in 1987 as a festival of non-aligned and other developing countries. I noticed the emphasis was on family values, and films of political differences were filtered out. The event lasted a full nine days. That year our Minister of Information and Broadcasting was inaugurating the event. The film selected was the Hindi comedy *Gol Maal*. The lead actor, Amol Palekar, came on screen speaking fluent Korean—dubbed, of course. It was a great joy to see the people in the jam-packed cinema house laughing and enjoying the film. Later that evening, during the dinner we had hosted for the minister at our residence, a Korean film star enquired, 'Mrs Sapra, how is Raju?' I had no clue who she was referring to. As far as I knew, there was no Indian actor named Raju. She went on to say she liked the song *Mera Joota Hai Japani*. It was then that I understood she is talking about Raj Kapoor. Of course, she would be familiar with him, given that Koreans watch many films from bygone eras. Over the years, I have observed that the love of Indian cinema is universal.

Continuing with the positive aspects of the diplomatic corps, in our lifetime we were able to witness events such as the 1982 Football World Cup in Spain, the 1988 Olympics in South Korea, the 2002 Commonwealth Games in Manchester and the 2006 Cricket World Cup in Trinidad and Tobago. Watching something up close and not on television is an entirely different experience.

As I mentioned earlier, very few diplomats have served in both North and South Korea. After the Second World War, Korea was divided into North and South along a truce line at 38 degrees latitude and that is what separates the two countries ever since. Our family has had the unique opportunity to visit the DMZ (demilitarised zone)—a 4 km wide by 248 km long stretch of land that separates the two countries—on two different occasions from both sides. The experiences in both places were very different even though the language was common.

I remember it was Chuseok in South Korea, the Korean equivalent of Thanksgiving when families get together to pay respects to their ancestors and also give thanks for an abundant autumn harvest. I never imagined that for our family it would be a very different kind of family get-together. It was our first year there and the diesel tank outside our house that provided fuel to keep the house warm ran out. Try to picture us living in an ice-cold house with only one electric heater in one of the bedrooms. Everything in the city had shut down for three days, leaving us with no means to get more diesel from any of the petrol pumps. Somehow, we managed to survive the first day, but the prospect of spending another two days with three small kids huddled together in one room was enough to drive anyone mad. Fortunately, our embassy handyman, Mr Kim, arrived the next day with cans of diesel. Don't ask me where he got them from.

North Korea was challenging but it made up for that in scenic beauty. Certain parts were breathtaking, especially the Kumgang Mountains (Diamond Mountains). We were taken by the Foreign Office to visit them, and once we reached the top there were small ponds all around. Wherever we go, I like to touch the water, so here was no exception. The area was a little slippery, and before I knew it, I had slipped into the water. The expressions on the faces of the Korean Foreign Office officials were priceless. With some help, I managed to come out of the water, soaking wet. After catching my breath and recovering from the shock and embarrassment of falling in, I smiled and nonchalantly declared that in India we try to take a dip in all holy water bodies. All three of my children burst out laughing. After checking that I hadn't broken any bones, the Koreans were pacified. The next time I visited that area was when the Foreign Office had taken all the heads of mission there. I observed that they had erected a railing around the ponds and put up signs to warn people. If you ever go there, remember that yours truly is responsible for the sign preventing you from getting near the water!

In 1989, Chung Ju-Yung, founder of the highly successful Hyundai Group, visited North Korea. He was born into a peasant family in 1918 in this region known for its beauty. He promised to fund a joint North–South tourism project at Mount Kumgang. Chung Ju-Yung returned to North Korea in 1998 and became the first civilian to cross the DMZ without an official escort since 1953. The North Korean government agreed to start the project that year. The division of the Korean peninsula in 1950 prevented South Koreans from visiting this beautiful region. On 14 November 1998, after nearly fifty years, the first ship bound for the tourism zone left South Korea on a twelve-hour voyage with 441 South Koreans on board. The ship docked at a port near Mount Kumgang. We were posted there during this period, and for me personally, it touched a nerve. Being a child of parents who were forced to move from Lahore to Delhi in 1947 and aware of the hardships my near and dear ones had to face, my heart went out to the Koreans. One of the consequences of the long conflict between the North Korea and South Korea was the separation of families. Millions of Koreans were separated when the border was drawn and sealed in 1953. Exchange of mail between the two countries is forbidden. In 1989, I remember reading about the Koreans in South Korea who were hopeful of meeting or receiving word from their families left behind in North Korea. After we left North Korea in 2000, we still took interest in what was happening in the region. Originally the tourists arrived by cruise ships, but now there is a road leading through the demilitarised zone. The family reunion centre has helped some families meet their loved ones. A few such incidents come to mind: An eighty-two-year-old South Korean lady said she could die in peace and without regrets after meeting her two younger sisters and brother. Kim Dong-yul left his wife and two-year-old daughter in North Korea in 1949. I wonder what he must have felt meeting his daughter after a period of sixty years.

As with all interconnected forces, where there is Yin, there is Yang. Moving, as I have already mentioned, is very stressful. Even now, I have nightmares in which we are leaving a place and there is still so much to be sorted out, or we are leaving tomorrow and nothing is packed. Sometimes, I still wake up in the middle of the night with palpitations and realise that phase of my life is over. Loneliness is a common thread across the diplomatic corps. In my case, being an only child made the absence of my parents and family members more pronounced. Not being there when a close family member—an uncle or an aunt whom I was close to growing up—passed away was painful. It takes a long time, sitting alone in a distant land, to recover.

The most difficult thing I found was not having the support of family when our daughter was born in Saudi Arabia, what with the postpartum depression and having to look after a one-year-old toddler and a newborn. I would have given my right arm to have my mother and aunts around me.

Then it's also about yourself and your own personal development. Being fond of teaching, it was a big challenge to find work in every new posting, and, every three years, having to leave behind something you enjoyed doing and start anew in another place. Having to prove yourself all over again every time is difficult. While we were posted in North Korea, leaving behind both our girls in Delhi for the first time was something that tore me apart inside. Our elder daughter was already in college and the younger one was preparing for her twelfth-grade board examinations. Not having any family member nearby made it difficult for her to focus on her exams. And we had to homeschool our eleven-year-old son because the schooling he was receiving at the local school was inadequate.

As my husband rose in seniority in the service, the responsibility of organising formal course dinners and luncheons became a source of stress that cannot be put into words—another recurring theme in my periodic nightmares. There you are, mingling with the guests while your mind is in the kitchen, worrying about whether all the instructions given earlier were being followed. A senior officer's wife once told me that a large number of spouses in our service suffered from diabetes.

Coming back to our children, it wasn't easy for them to move, leave behind friends and adapt to new schools and education systems. One of our daughters was once asked, 'All this moving around must have been exciting,' to which she responded: 'I will never put my children through what our parents subjected us to.' As a parent, it hurt a bit when she said that.

One ponders and asks oneself: Was it worth it? If I had to do it all over again, would I be party to it? Not all spouses in the service would reply in the affirmative. There have been cases of spouses not being able to cope with the challenges and hurdles we face, which is very sad and something we as an IFS family need to address. The reason I would willingly do it again is because of all the beautiful memories sealed in my mind. The opportunity to see new places, meet interesting people and forge lasting friendships with some of them is invaluable to me.

I have been challenged to teach English as a second language across various educational levels, from kindergarten and middle school to polytechnic college, catering to students of all ages from five to seventy. Notably, among the senior adults I've taught English to were the spouses of Ambassadors in North Korea. Not being able to understand the language spoken can be frustrating. For many of the wives, English was a hurdle and helping them learn was a rewarding experience for me. It was so much fun setting up the lesson plans while keeping in mind food from different places, clothing and places of interest in their countries, to name a few. In the end, it's been a learning curve as I stepped out of the house in each posting and immersed myself in the local sights and sounds. Drawing energy from different places has been enriching and rewarding. Making lemonade when life gave me lemons has been crucial. Adapting and remaining positive helped. As an Ambassador's wife from another country put it, we create mini versions of our countries in distant lands, showcasing our cultures, history and food. Personally, I would say we do this for love at all levels, starting foremost with our families. Correct me if I am wrong, but love is all you need at the end of the day.

A Country Like No Other
Brazil

SHRIMI SINHA

After settling down in Delhi following my husband's retirement, I look back and marvel at the wonderful life we led, the amazing experiences and the great friends we made along the way. The life of a diplomatic spouse has been aptly described in Reba Som's book *Hop, Skip and Jump*. This is true for all diplomatic spouses, especially those from India. Every three years, we have to pack our bags, shop for Indian spices and cereals, look for new domestic staff to accompany us and head to another corner of the planet. Our jumps are across continents to distant lands and unfamiliar cultures. Packing to leave is always a heart-wrenching experience. It was especially so for our most distant posting, Brazil.

When we got posted to Brasilia in 1999, after our stint in Geneva, we were rather apprehensive at first, as it was so far away. There were no direct flights from India to Brazil; one had to fly to New York, spend a night there and then fly to São Paolo or Rio de Janeiro. From there, one took a domestic flight to Brasilia.

We were overjoyed about the layover in New York, as it gave us the opportunity to meet our elder son who was studying in the US. As for Brazil, I knew precious little about it. I had only heard of the famous Copacabana Beach, the Sugarloaf Mountain, Pelé, samba and, of course, the numerous Miss Worlds it had produced over the years. Our younger son was very excited at the thought of getting to meet his favourite football players—the three Rs—Ronaldo, Rivaldo and Roberto Carlos.

Looking out of the aircraft window as we landed in Brasilia, all we could see was a drab and arid place, not half as beautiful as I expected it to be. The red soil gave it a rugged look, but the lack of tree cover was jarring.

Brasilia was planned by the government as a new capital for Brazil to encourage people to move away from the coastal areas where they had settled after migrating from Europe to the interior. The city was designed by Oscar Niemeyer in the shape of an aircraft. Niemeyer, a pupil of Le Corbusier who had planned Chandigarh, placed the parliament and the presidential palace in the cockpit, with government offices on both sides of the aisle. The TV tower was built at the rear, surrounded by a large open space. The residential apartments, Asa Norte and Asa Sul, were located on the two wings. They were dull multi-storeyed structures that reminded me of the apartment buildings in the old communist East Germany.

In front of the aircraft, an artificial lake had been formed by damming a small stream. Across it were the bungalows of wealthier residents in the areas of Lago Norte and Lago Sul.

Artisans from neighbouring localities would gather in the field around the TV tower every weekend to sell beautiful lacework, embroidered items, paintings and many other handicrafts. I loved exploring the different stalls and ending up at the food vendors. The first time we went there, I was drawn to a pakora-like dish being cooked by ladies from the province of Bahia. This was the popular acarajé, a ball of mashed black-eyed peas, deep-fried, then split in half and stuffed with a spicy paste of cashew and prawns, and served with hot sauce. Being Indian, I was very confident I could deal with the spice, but I was soon rushing to the closest cold drinks stall, where I gulped down copious amounts of Coke. I eventually learnt to respect Bahian food which, like the people of the province, has roots in Western Africa. However, that was the last time I ate acarajé.

We settled down in our house in Lago Sul and our son was admitted to ninth grade at the American School. He also joined a tennis academy not far from home. It was started by a lady who had studied in the US on a tennis scholarship. When she returned, she set up her own tennis school. Brazilians are very sporty, and there was a string of clubs around the lake with large open lawns, offering excellent facilities and coaching for various sports. The same was true for gyms, which were scattered throughout the residential areas. Despite the variety of games, people were obsessed with football. Similar to how animated sports commentary in Hindi can be, in Brazil, when a goal was scored, the commentator would shout 'gooooooooal' for as long as he could hold his breath. I remember when Brazil won the World Cup in 2002, the players were flown to Brasilia in an aircraft that circled over the city several times to announce their arrival. They were then taken on an open bus all around the city, receiving a tumultuous welcome from adoring fans. It was an event I will never forget.

Language was a problem initially, but I soon learnt to speak 'passable' Portuguese after joining the language class organised at the embassy. It was enough for me to communicate with my house help, Marcelia, and for shopping. I discovered Brazilians were very familiar with my family name Sinha. 'Sinya' was used as a respectful form of address for a woman, a colloquial form of 'signora'.

I found Brazilian women to be open, lively, liberal-minded and quite uninhibited. They were also obsessed with beauty and their bodies. Seeing the super slim Brazilian women in their itsy-bitsy clothes had me rushing to the nearest gym and taking a year's membership. I not only lost a lot of weight but also made many wonderful friends there, who invited me to their beautifully kept homes and included me in their activities.

One day, after our gym class, I asked a friend why she had not been coming the past few weeks. She explained that she had gone to São Paolo to have liposuction on her tummy. She then started discussing the operation and everyone else chipped in with their own experiences. I was struck by their openness to discussing such personal matters and a bit puzzled by their willingness to undergo cosmetic surgeries despite being so slim and fit. I suppose their chiselled bodies were the result of both exercise and surgery.

The lack of inhibition was prevalent even in the schools in Brazil. One would think that schools would enforce a certain level of decorum in their students' dresses. Imagine my shock on my first visit to the school when I saw some girls in skimpy clothes. Further shock awaited me when our son, who was in the tenth grade, asked me to buy a gift for his classmate's baby. She had recently become a mother, and the father of the child was in twelfth grade. I was not surprised when our Belgian friend who has two daughters—one in the same class as our son—was thrilled to get posted to Saudi Arabia.

Unlike many other South American countries, Brazil's economy was quite stable in those days. The country is famous for its semiprecious stones and crystals. I loved visiting the jewellery shop in Asa Sul, which was favoured by many in the diplomatic corps, to look at their new designs. Thanks to the many special offers at the store, we picked up quite a few pieces. For crystals, we would drive to Crystalina, a dusty little town about two to three hours from Brasilia. There were many shops selling quartz crystals in the form of decorative items like birds, rocks, etc. We picked up a few for ourselves but mostly bought them as gifts to bring back home.

Brazil is a delight for fruits and vegetables, not to mention all kinds of meats. They were abundant and reasonably priced. We would invariably return home with a crate of oranges or other fruits, not just a kilo or two like we used to in earlier postings. People rarely paid the full amount in shops or supermarkets. They would pay in instalments not only for shoes, handbags, mobiles and household items but also for basic items like bread, milk and yoghurt.

Restaurants were aplenty and not too expensive, especially the churrascarias, which offered Brazil's traditional barbeques. Feijoada is Brazil's most popular dish. This stew is loaded with black beans and a variety of meats served over rice, with greens on the side. It was too heavy for my Indian stomach, so I steered clear of it after trying it a few times. Caipirinha is a popular drink enjoyed by Brazilians in large quantities. It is made with cachaça, a type of Brazilian rum, mixed with crushed lime and sugar. It is delicious but very strong. Pão de queijo is a tapioca cheese ball served as a snack. I continue to make it even now. Maracujá mousse is a popular Brazilian dessert that is so easy to make it became a staple at my later postings.

I found most of the working-class people to be a happy go lucky lot. With food being so affordable and healthcare taken care of by the government, it was no wonder they didn't believe in saving for the future. I didn't see a single hungry person in my three years in Brasilia. However, there was definitely a divide between the rich and the poor. The working staff lived in satellite towns and were provided subsidised buses to commute to their place of work. In Rio de Janeiro, the poor lived in favelas, which had amenities like TVs, washing machines and cooking stoves. And this was in the year 2000.

Carnivals are a big thing in Brazil. Held in the month of February, Carnival marks the beginning of the austere forty-day Lent period until Easter, during which meat is not eaten. It is celebrated in several towns, but the one in Rio is the biggest, with a different theme each year. A special stadium has been built for this event. Since plane fares were very expensive, we decided to take an overnight bus to watch it. We arrived a few days earlier to see the other attractions in Rio. It was amazing to go up the Corcovado hill and see the statue of Christ the Redeemer up close. We also took the cable car to the top of Sugarloaf Mountain and enjoyed a breathtaking view of Rio below.

I can't say the same for our walk on Copacabana Beach. Instead of savouring the stroll and admiring the view, we were constantly glancing left and right to steer clear of anyone walking too close, as we had been warned about the many pickpockets there. Next to Copacabana Beach is Ipanema Beach, which is much longer and less crowded. It became more famous after Frank Sinatra's iconic song *The Girl from Ipanema*.

For the Carnival, the participating samba schools prepare tableaus based on a common theme. The year we went, the theme was India. This was because, for several centuries, Brazil was a stopover in the Portuguese Empire, where ships docked on their way to Goa. India had an exotic image in Brazil, so the Carnival's theme gave them an opportunity to depict lavish Indian maharajas and garishly underdressed dancing girls. Even ordinary people could participate in the Carnival by signing up with one of the participating samba schools. The Rio Carnival has come to symbolise Brazil worldwide.

After a year into our stay, we decided to travel around. Eight of us from the Indian Embassy hired a van with a driver for a week-long trip to Iguaçu Falls. We drove through the countryside, stopping at various places for meals and finally halting for the night at a farm. Iguaçu Falls, located at the tri-junction of Brazil, Argentina and Paraguay, is regarded as one of the seven wonders of nature. Up to 7,000 cubic metres of water falls every second, making it the most extensive waterfall system in the world. There are several waterfalls in close proximity, the most spectacular of which is called the Devil's Throat.

By our third year, low-cost airlines had begun operating in Brazil. We flew over the Amazon to Manaus, the capital of the vast state of Amazonas. Situated in the heart of the Amazon rainforest, one could only reach there by flight or by boat. We stayed at a nature resort inside the forest. On the first day, we took a walking tour through the lush vegetation of the forest. The next day, we went on a boat ride on the Negro River. Young boys in smaller boats would approach us, holding snakes of all sizes, alligators and exotic birds. They would ask us to touch and hold these animals. I don't remember much of the boat ride after that. It was only after seeing the photos that I realised I had my head down, eyes shut and ears covered throughout the ride, because I was petrified. There are photos of Dilip and our sons with snakes around their necks and holding a sloth. This boat ride is certainly not for the faint-hearted like me.

Although Brazil is predominantly a Catholic country, the people are tolerant and open to all religions. In Brasilia, a temple has been constructed that does not belong to any particular religion. It features a high spiral over a circular hall with a large crystal at the top. There are no religious symbols or idols inside, no prayers are performed and no music is played. People just sit in silent meditation.

We were once invited to a place on the outskirts of Brasilia where around fifty Brazilians were celebrating Mahashivratri. They sat in a large hall dressed in white kurta-pyjamas, chanting 'Om Namah Shivaya' along with a tape recording left behind by a visiting Indian saint.

While we were there (1999–2002), trade with India was just picking up. Indian pharmaceuticals and diesel were slowly finding a market in Brazil. The Brazilian government provided free medicines to its people and the cost of AIDS medicine imported from Western countries was becoming prohibitive. Brazil's health minister visited India and identified a few companies whose medicines were approved for purchase by his government.

Life in Brasilia was leisurely. There were few delegations from India, which was a big relief after Geneva. There were just about half a dozen Indian families, all of them professionals, mainly teaching technical subjects at the university. Most of our official entertaining was with the diplomatic community that was small and close-knit.

After three years, it was time for us to leave. With a heavy heart and tears in my eyes, I bid farewell to my Brazilian and Indian friends, as well as to friends from the diplomatic corps.

Memories of an Accidental Diplomatic Spouse

AJAY SHANKAR

I first met Meera when we joined as probationers at the charming campus of the Lal Bahadur Shastri National Academy of Administration in Mussoorie. One of its traditions was for probationers to stage plays. I volunteered. So did Meera. We ended up working together in two plays, acting and directing. Our lifelong journey together began in theatre. We were soon enjoying the evening beauty of Mussoorie in the monsoons and going on to have dinners at Whispering Windows.

By the time Meera was getting ready to go overseas, we decided to get married—a decision more of the heart than of the head. A well-meaning relative enquired whether Meera would resign and be the 'dutiful good wife'. The more common query was whether we had thought through the implications of sustaining a marriage while remaining in our respective services. When I look back now, I think we have been exceptionally fortunate. Not being ambitious or craving conventional success helped, although we did our work as well as we could and derived a sense of fulfilment from it. Our self-esteem was high, which made us indifferent to the perceptions of 'doing well' in our fiercely competitive services, and also enabled unconventional choices. I came to Delhi as an Under Secretary, which was not considered normal. Then I volunteered to work for the 9th Asian Games in 1982 in order to spend more time in the city, against the advice of well-wishers who claimed that IAS officers did not make a mark by organising games and that I would be risking a blot on my career if things did not go well, as seemed quite likely. As it turned out, the Asian Games were an extraordinary success.

I also did not hesitate to take leave to join Meera overseas during her postings. She also chose to spend more time at the headquarters in Delhi so that we could be together. A close friend gingerly enquired why, unlike her batchmates, Meera was not overseas as an Ambassador. I quipped, 'She prefers the dubious pleasure of my company to being Her Excellency.' During the periods when we had to stay apart, we experienced the wisdom of the saying 'absence makes the heart grow fonder'.

I first took leave to join Meera on her first posting to Germany. After being received at the Indian Consulate in Frankfurt, I was escorted to the railway station and put on the train for Lüneburg, where Meera was learning German. My escort informed the family in my coach that I did not know German and requested if they could ensure that I got off at Lüneburg. The German family had a teenage son who knew English, and he became the translator. The mother enquired how I would manage after I got off the train at Lüneburg. I replied that I would be received by my wife. The puzzled expression on her face changed to one of enlightened understanding as she said, 'Oh, they have child marriages in India, don't they?' And here I was, a twenty-six-year-old who had been a magistrate!

Meera moved on to the Indian Consulate in Hamburg, a delightful port city which, strangely enough, prided itself on being very English. For me, an interesting discovery was that stereotypes do have some basis. The sight of Germans polishing their cars on the weekend, even when it was drizzling, made no sense to my Indian eyes. Once, as I was leaving the counter of a store after paying, the overstuffed plastic bag gave way and the groceries, including a bottle of juice that broke, were strewn on the floor. The woman behind the counter rushed over to pick up things. It took me a while to realise that she had not come to help me but to clean the floor and restore it to its shining, polished state! The discipline of German drivers is such that autobahns still do not have speed limits. This driving discipline became so ingrained in me that when we drove to Paris, I found myself muttering like a German about how badly the Parisians drive. To complete the experience, as I was leaving a store, I saw a young lady gently reversing into my car to push it back slightly, creating space for her car to exit. She waved at me with a smile as she noticed the alarm on my face.

I discovered how people in public interactions react according to stereotypes. I picked up some German and tried to use it in shops. I was invariably mistaken for a poor immigrant, a Turkish Gastarbeiter (guest worker), and treated with marked condescension. After some time, I thought I would adopt a different approach: speak in English with an American accent and ask confidently whether I could pay with my American Express card. The change was dramatic. The salesperson would try to communicate in broken English with the deference due to the rich American tourist, albeit a brown one of slender build. Years later, when I was much older, the extra security checks I often underwent at airports seemed more suited to screening a potential terrorist—strange for someone as mild-looking as me!

When Meera went to the US to head the commercial wing at the Indian Embassy, I took study leave and accompanied her. By this time, economists were beginning to take over the world as the new 'Brahmins'. I had studied and taught political science in Allahabad, so I decided to challenge myself. I wrote the GRE examination, joined the graduate school at Georgetown University and picked up a master's degree in economics in my early forties. I would attend classes and then disappear without hanging around. It took a while before I became friends with my classmates. They later told me they had speculated about my age and felt I was probably nearing thirty, which I found quite flattering. They thought I was quite eccentric for punishing myself with the rigours of graduate school even though I had a secure job.

I became the visible parent of our daughter, Priya, who joined Grade II at the neighbourhood elementary school, as Meera's work schedule turned out to be heavy and demanding. I used to be the only father among mothers waiting to meet the teacher or dropping off and picking up their children to and from birthday parties. Judging by the expressions on some of the mothers' faces, I wondered if they thought I was a single parent struggling to raise my daughter and, to make matters worse, possibly unemployed. Over time, I got to know the mothers of Priya's friends well. Priya, our only child, was quite shy initially. My first meeting with her class teacher was extraordinary. She lectured me that she understood Asian mores were different and that we valued obedience and discipline and instilled it in our children, but emphasised that we should encourage Priya to act more freely and become more American. I realised it would be pointless to explain to her that Priya had not known scolding or strict discipline but was just naturally quiet and well-behaved. I mumbled something to the effect of 'Yes, ma'am. I understand. We will try', and left.

Gradually, Priya adjusted, made friends and became popular in school. Then there was an extraordinary incident when she was in Grade V. I have a sweet tooth. I came home to find some cookies in the kitchen, tasted one, liked it and ate all of them. When Priya found out what had happened, she was inconsolable. I had eaten up her 'school project'. She was the team leader of a class group that was to design an advertising campaign for these cookies, targeting older people. I had to send a plaintive note to her teacher, explaining what had happened and asking for help. She sent a sweet reply, telling me about the speciality Jewish store where I could buy the same cookies. My relationship with Priya escaped an irreparable rupture!

Priya's school was a revelation. As soon as she entered Grade II, she had to borrow books of her level from the public library and answer simple questions after reading them. The school was in a traditional Jewish neighbourhood, so we learnt about Jewish festivals like Hanukkah, which I had not heard of before. Priya even became an honorary Jew for some time, as her name became Priyah until they got the spelling right in her class. They were constantly engaged in interesting projects. The children had to present their innovations to their class in front of all the parents and compete for a prize. Some of the children were amazingly creative, thinking of practical solutions to improve their lives. One boy had come up with a way of retrieving morning newspapers without going out in the cold by adapting a fishing rod. Picking up the skills of earning money through yard sales at home or selling food made with the help of parents at school fundraisers was normal. Additionally, they performed a scene from one of Shakespeare's classics at the prestigious Folger Theatre.

I thought I knew America well, having read so many books and seen many films set there. But there were surprises. My first bit of education came within weeks of moving there. At parties hosted by diplomats, some overlap in guestlists is natural. When I met the same couple at a second party, I ventured to ask the lady the polite question of what her husband did. She snapped at me, stating he was not her husband. I learnt my lesson! The term 'partner' was becoming increasingly common. Meera began sending some of her invitations to Mr/Ms … and Partner.

I had grown up reading thrillers where the heroes always had bourbon on the rocks and martinis over lunch, and watching films where the hero would light his cigarette like the 'Marlboro man'. To my utter surprise, I found that this America had become history. Most American guests at our parties would have a glass or two of wine and some, a vodka. Smoking earned you public disapproval, and you had to light your cigarette furtively in open spaces. On one occasion, a dear friend visited during an official trip. I took him shopping for Western classical music CDs to a mall after he had finished his day's work. Dressed in a suit with a bow tie and a pipe in hand, he cut a striking figure. He lit his pipe, and we entered a store. A young salesgirl screamed at him. My friend could not comprehend a word due to her distinct Southern accent until I translated. She was saying, 'Get out! Get out! You can't smoke in here!' I quickly caught his hand and dragged my traumatised friend out of the shop.

I also discovered how social interactions were so important for diplomats. I learnt the art of walking up to a stranger, introducing myself and then navigating my way towards an interesting conversation. I found that being the diplomatic spouse often evoked considerable curiosity. I often say that the Indian Foreign Service is such a good career: you are a part of the social elite wherever you serve; representing India gets you more attention than your counterparts from smaller countries; and you have the satisfaction of serving your country in critical ways. I also got a glimpse of the substantial work that is facilitated over dinners and lunches, as well as how difficult it is for diplomats to achieve favourable outcomes, requiring patience, persistence and innovative approaches. We were fortunate to live in a charming house and to be able to host a wide range of interesting people.

Meera served as Ambassador to Germany and then to the US. I could join her in Germany only for short periods. After retirement, I moved to Washington. Before leaving for Berlin, the German Ambassador in Delhi had invited Meera to dinner and briefed us about the differences in dinner etiquette between the two countries. In India, you did not know when, or even whether, guests would come, but you were sure they would leave as soon as they had finished eating. In Germany, it was the other way around; you could be sure that they would arrive within five minutes of the time given in the invitation, but you could not be sure when they would leave. Sure enough, the Germans were invariably on time, even waiting outside for a few minutes to ensure punctuality, and they enjoyed their post-dinner coffee, liqueur and leisurely conversation.

I'd like to share an extraordinary experience. In a select dinner conversation where the ninety-year-old former German Chancellor Helmut Schmidt was present, the question of what the biggest global risk was went around the table. Various opinions were voiced by the guests that included Amartya Sen and Ingvar Kamprad, the founder of Ikea, and us. Schmidt, who had been silently inhaling snuff and smoking non-stop, was prophetic in his reply: the risk to the world economy from the collapse of one of the unregulated hedge funds—and this was a whole year and a half before the global financial crisis!

It so happened that Prime Minister Manmohan Singh was visiting Berlin when I was there. Meera told me the convention is that the Ambassador's spouse accompanies the prime minister's wife. I was glad to follow the unwritten rule, and found myself accompanying Mrs Singh to her programmes, the most memorable part of which was a visit to a small pristine medieval town with cobbled streets (probably renovated). The guide, a German woman, educated us about the special relationship the Germans have with beer. It was the first certified drink after the plague took a heavy toll on human lives during the early Middle Ages. Beer was even given to crying babies to calm them; it was considered highly nutritious and a complete food. The beer belly was a result of sausages and pork, with beer thought to be benign, and it was widely believed that getting drunk on beer once a month was the key to longevity and good health. I became an admirer of Mrs Singh, who heard all this with a diplomatic straight face without any comment.

The cultural contrast between the German and American elites was sharp. A formal dinner in Germany would often be held in a historic building with traditional décor. It would begin with a short classical music piece and then a long, scholarly speech. In America, a dinner speech had to have jokes. I remember attending an award ceremony for outstanding young scientists where the scientific advisor to the president began his speech with the quip that there was now a new definition of middle age: it was from sixty to seventy-five, and he was only seventy-one!

America had substantially changed since we were last there in the early 1990s. It had surprised the world by electing the charismatic Barack Obama as its first Black president. Women had broken glass ceilings. Hillary Clinton was Secretary of State and, but for Obama, may have been President. Women held the positions of Under Secretary in the State and Defence departments. (In the early 1990s, Meera would often be mistaken for the personal assistant who should be taking notes and not speaking.) Indian Americans had arrived. I remember accompanying Meera on a freezing day to the oath-taking ceremony of the young Nikki

Haley, the daughter of Sikh immigrants, who had just been elected as the Republican governor of South Carolina. In her inaugural speech, she drew attention to her Indian origin with pride.

Being the Ambassador's husband immediately after retiring as a Secretary looking after industry in the Government of India was quite enjoyable. I had all the privileges of being the spouse without any of the burdens, as I was incapable of being the 'good wife'. I was glad to see respect for public service in society. Anyone who served as an Ambassador of the US carried the title for the rest of their life. I found myself becoming Secretary Shankar, rather than a former 'babu', with its somewhat pejorative connotations in India.

For some time, I was a public policy scholar at the Woodrow Wilson International Center for Scholars. This gave me an inside view of the depth of American think tanks, some with close ties to one party and some with another. The rich flow of papers and ideas within the policy establishment was an eye-opener. It made me wish we had more of this in India and within our political parties. Discussions on the economic prognosis for the parts of the world I knew so little about—Latin America, Africa, Eastern Europe—and global economic policy and management issues were extremely interesting.

I have many extraordinarily memories as a diplomatic spouse. One is of former California Governor Jerry Brown telling Meera that he had the unenviable task of telling Californians, who had just elected him after a long gap that they needed to work harder, earn less and pay more taxes. There was the high point of going to the private upstairs portion of the White House where Prime Minister Manmohan Singh and his family were hosted for a private reception by the then US President Barack Obama and his wife before the state dinner. The only Americans present were the then vice president Joe Biden and his wife, the Secretary of

State Hillary Clinton and the National Security Advisor General James L. Jones. I remember Biden telling Meera that she was the most important Ambassador in town. In the protocol of Western countries, the Ambassador ranks just after the visiting head of state or government. During the Obamas' visit to India, we accompanied them to the house where Mahatma Gandhi had stayed in Mumbai and saw how he was such an inspirational figure for them. Then, we visited a school where the students persuaded the Obamas to join them on the dance floor. Barack admitted candidly that this was an area where Michelle was clearly better!

As I look back from the leisure of retirement, I am glad that Meera and I met fifty years ago by accident, had the confidence to follow our hearts and have had a wonderful life together. I enjoyed every moment of being a diplomatic spouse.

The Spouse Route

ASHOK PANDEY

When I wrote the civil services exam, I wanted to join only the Indian Administrative Service, and I was successful in my goal. And years later, I married a woman from the foreign service. But then, *c'est la vie*.

Initially, my cadre was Assam and Meghalaya. Later, due to personal reasons, I had my cadre changed to Bihar. In my various capacities, particularly as an officer in the Ministry of Commerce, I had the opportunity to visit several countries.

I met my wife, Reena Poovaiah, when we were undergoing a diploma course in French at the Institute of Foreign Languages in New Delhi. The Ministry of External Affairs had assigned French as a compulsory foreign language to Reena. The institute came under my charge because I was then the chief administrative officer in the Ministry of Defence. The teachers, particularly those of French, were fairly close to me and persuaded me to learn the language at their institute, and I relented.

Later, I met Reena's brother, who was a young army officer, and we all became friends. My first wife, Manju, our son, Amit, and daughters, Shailaja and Sujata, also got to know Reena and her family well. We remained connected even when Reena was away on her foreign postings. She also knew my parents, siblings and my in-laws. My children, from a young age, looked upon Reena as one of their favourite aunts.

I lost Manju in a tragic car accident in Kolkata, and my children and I were left shattered. Reena, at that time, was posted in Kathmandu. She was a fount of solace for my daughters, who often stayed with her during their vacations. Her cheerful and positive attitude gave us courage and comfort. While serving as a member of the Bihar State Electricity Board, I, too, had several occasions to visit Kathmandu.

During one of my visits to city, a friend with whom I was staying, in a surprising move, took me to their then prime minister, G.P. Koirala. We discussed some issues related to India and Nepal, particularly his worry regarding the supply of energy from Bihar. I conveyed to him that Bihar and Nepal could provide energy to each other in areas that were deficient in power on either side of the border. In any case, there was an existing arrangement, it only had to be strengthened and implemented. He was happy with my constructive suggestion, which was later taken seriously and acted upon.

Meanwhile, my son had got into the Indian Railway Traffic Service and began his training. My older daughter was pursuing her bachelor's degree at Lady Shri Ram College, and my youngest daughter had just appeared for the tenth standard exams. As time passed, we all got closer to Reena. It seemed natural to take the next step and marry her. In 1993, soon after she was posted back to Delhi from Kathmandu, we got married.

I, too, was deputed from Bihar to the Lok Sabha Secretariat as Secretary to the Speaker, Shivraj Patil. I had worked with him earlier, serving as his special assistant when he was with the Ministry of Defence and Commerce. He was instrumental in getting me back to Delhi. To be in the Lok Sabha Secretariat and assist such a knowledgeable and dignified Speaker was educational.

In 1996, the then Foreign Secretary, Salman Haidar, sent Reena on deputation to the Prime Minister's Residence Office on 7, Race Course Road, as Director of Hospitality. The newly appointed Prime Minister H.D. Deve Gowda had come from Karnataka and was residing there with his family. I was happy about this, as it meant Reena could continue to be in Delhi. She was there from 1996 to 1999, serving two more prime ministers, I.K. Gujral and Atal Bihari Vajpayee. All three were extremely polite and, indeed, perfect gentlemen. Reena got along well with them and their families, and we kept in touch even later.

In December of 1999, Reena was posted to the High Commission in London and headed the economic and commercial wing. I accompanied her. The house given to us was located in Finchley Central and belonged to a fine Chinese gentleman whose support made our stay rather comfortable.

Postings abroad provide a unique opportunity to interact with various sections of society. We fully utilised this and developed friendships with people of different nationalities. Reena stayed in London for about three years, and during that period she made two trips to India. I also got the opportunity to visit London three times during her tenure, with some official delegations. I took great interest in all activities and never missed a chance to attend meetings related to public interest, particularly pertaining to our Indian diaspora, but since I was still in service, I had to return to Delhi.

I recall a trip to London for a conference of speakers from the Commonwealth nations, where I had the occasion to meet distinguished speakers and officers from various countries. I even had multiple opportunities to meet Her Majesty The Queen. During the conference, I developed a strong equation with several leaders, including some of Indian origin. These relationships endured as we continued to meet at conferences in various countries thereafter.

After some time, I retired and had plenty of time to spend in London. My usual routine was to leave home after breakfast or lunch and spend my time walking around the area near the High Commission, which was very well situated. Many places worth seeing were usually within walking distance. I also spent a few hours in the library of the High Commission and, on occasion, lunched with Mahesh Nathani, the then Head of the Chancery. After lunch, we would go for a rather scenic walk along the bank of River Thames.

I was also part of an informal group that included a minister from the High Commission, a resident correspondent of a leading Indian newspaper and an old friend from India settled in London. We called ourselves the 'Khichdi Biryani Club'.

From London, I made trips to Delhi to meet my children and their families. I also visited Bangalore, Mumbai and Patna frequently to meet our friends and members of extended family. During my time in Delhi, I was associated with numerous cultural and social organisations, and spent most of my time there.

While in London, we travelled extensively throughout the United Kingdom and enjoyed every moment, especially during the weekends. Another cherished memory was celebrating the dawn of the millennium year, 2000, at the High Commission.

After completing her tenure in London, Reena was transferred as Consul General to the wonderful city of Istanbul. Khushwant

Singh described it as one of the best cities in the world, as it offered everything one could imagine. It was considered a wonderful blend of ancient and modern treasures.

On our arrival, we were mesmerised by the place. We enjoyed every single moment, although in the beginning I had my reservations that our house was part of the residence where the owners of the house also lived. I thought we would have a tough time with them, but as the months passed we developed a deep bond.

Our floor was fully independent with an exquisite garden, a swimming pool and a huge balcony. Just across the road was the lovely Bosphorus Strait, winding its way from the Sea of Marmara to the Black Sea. From our windows, we could enjoy lovely views of boats, cruises, ships, oil tankers and submarines passing through the Bosphorus. The sight of dolphins playfully leaping in the water filled our hearts with immense delight.

Istanbul has the unique distinction of falling in two continents, Asia and Europe. Our residence was situated in the European part, and just across the Bosphorus lay the Asian part of the city. We visited the other side frequently, particularly for its culinary delicacies and to meet friends.

I continued with the routine of dividing my time between Istanbul and Delhi. I remember once I was delayed in returning to Istanbul. It seems my wife's driver was missing me somewhat and told her that if 'Babu Sir' (a name by which Reena lovingly calls me) came by the fifteenth of that month, it would be fine, but after that 'if he come or no come' it won't matter to him. This was very endearing to me.

Istanbul was such a glamorous city that consulates of several countries were located there. This led to a regular series of receptions, lunches, cocktails, dinners and cultural events. We enjoyed every single moment and made plenty of friends, one being our landlady who was extremely fond of reading and talking. Many evenings were spent together during 'Happy Hours', watching the beauty of the sun setting over the Bosphorus. Although she has passed away now, her entire family became close to us, and fortunately the relationship continues to this day.

After completing her tenure in Istanbul in 2005, Reena was posted as Ambassador to Armenia, another lovely country. It didn't take us long to feel settled in Yerevan, the capital city. The guards and local house help were extremely polite and dependable. Unfortunately, we couldn't say the same for the Indian house help we had taken with us to Istanbul and Yerevan. Due to a few incidents, he had to be repatriated.

I found the country very interesting and toured it extensively. I used to go for long walks whenever I desired. The winter in Yerevan was much harsher than in London and Istanbul, but summer was generally pleasant, except for a few days when the temperature rose to about 50°C. But due to the agreeable mornings and evenings, the heat never bothered us much.

I soon fell into a routine of visiting the libraries at the embassy and the American University of Armenia. There was an extremely helpful librarian at the university, Bella Avakian. With her help, I sat there and studied for hours on end. Bella and her husband, Aram, soon became close friends and we often toured Armenia together.

Another close friend with whom we spent time was Bushra Halepota, a Pakistani lady serving as the representative of the United Nations High Commissioner for Refugees (UNHCR). As we were preparing to leave for Delhi, Bushra enquired if I had any unfulfilled wishes in Armenia. I semi-seriously told her that I had three: a visit to one of her refugee camps, a massage in a salon and a visit to a decent nightclub. The very next day, she took me to an extremely well-managed refugee camp. Two days later, she arranged a massage appointment at a salon. I was thrilled by the thoughtfulness of the masseuse, who played a recorded sitar recital by Pandit Ravi Shankar especially for me. It was perfectly timed, ending just as my hour-long massage finished. The very next day, Bushra took us to a decent nightclub where we watched a few dances and then went on to have dinner.

Another person with whom we developed a strong friendship was Ambassador Terhi Hakala of Finland, a wonderful woman who served as a non-resident Ambassador to Armenia, Georgia and Azerbaijan. Upon our return to Delhi, by a happy coincidence, she was posted as Ambassador to India. To this day, we continue to remain in touch.

Reena was also accredited as Ambassador to Georgia. Tbilisi, the capital city, is an exotic place that is now rapidly gaining popularity as a destination for weddings and Indian film shoots. I thoroughly enjoyed the three-and-a-half-hour drive from Yerevan to Tbilisi through winding roads across the Caucasus Mountains. Our driver loved playing popular Hindi songs while driving. On our way, we would stop by the river in a quaint town called Dilijan in Armenia and relish a tasty meal of trout, salads, bread and fruits. Another simple pleasure was stopping by the wayside to eat corn on the cob.

We invariably stayed at the Marriott Hotel in Tbilisi. As always, we enjoyed interacting with the locals and made many friends there too, including a wonderful artist, the head of the chamber of commerce and an interesting professor, Dr Giuli Alasania. She was the mother of the then President, M. Saakashvili. A historian and professor at Tbilisi State University, she was studying the linkages between Georgian and Indian communities. She kindly invited us to visit a beautiful lodge set in a green, forested area about an hour's drive from Tbilisi. It was indeed a memorable visit. Reena and I went with our local Georgian interpreter, Tea. Dr Alasania had organised an exclusive lunch for us, with vintage wines, set out in a spectacular dining room under a gorgeous chandelier. As is customary in Armenia and Georgia, our driver was also seated with us at the same table.

Georgia is renowned for its wines and champagnes, which are immensely popular in Russia as well. The food is also delicious and a particular dish, Khachapuri, is the national favourite. One of the most intriguing places I visited was the birthplace of Joseph Stalin, former president of the Soviet Union. He was born in Gori, Georgia, in a humble two-room house. His parents were poor ethnic Georgians.

We were amazed by the number of Indian medical students in both the countries. While we were in Armenia, around 750 Indian students were studying at the Yerevan State Medical University (YSMU), including a few female students. The Armenians were quite fond of the Indian students because they learnt the local language quickly and were generally well behaved. Armenian is an Indo-European language, and historically its vocabulary shows traces of Iranian languages. Many similar words are also present in Hindi. Some Indian students married Armenian girls and returned with them to India. I remember Reena and I attended a convocation at the university where an Indian boy and girl delivered speeches in fluent Armenian. The rector and other members of the faculty looked on proudly. The Indian Embassy kept in touch with the students, as sometimes there were problems that needed sorting out.

In Tbilisi, there were then around 450 Indian medical students. Now, I am told, there are around 3,000 students in Yerevan and 11,000 in Georgia.

I was always interested in academics, having commenced my career with teaching. Thanks to amazing professors like Dr Akile Gürsoy in Istanbul and Dr Victoria Areklova in Yerevan, I had several occasions to address university students on subjects like Indology and parliamentary practices. In Tbilisi, I was requested to teach Hindi as a professor. I enjoyed it but could not become a regular.

After an extremely satisfying stay in Yerevan, with frequent visits to Tbilisi, we had to return to Delhi, as Reena retired in 2009. She, of course, had a remarkable tenure, both professionally and personally, in the foreign service. I, too, felt highly enriched by learning so much through my experiences of residing in these lovely countries.

In February 2010, we shifted to our apartment in Gurgaon. Although retired, Reena was re-employed as a consultant for Eurasia at the Ministry of External Affairs, until she decided to leave after four and a half years to enjoy retirement.

Our stay in all the four countries Reena was posted to after our wedding was useful and rewarding. An important part of our time abroad was the presence of my mother-in-law, Juby Poovaiah. After Reena's father passed away in 2002, she came to stay with us in London and remained with us until she passed away in December 2009. Her presence provided great stability and warmth, especially when I was back in Delhi for short spells. She attracted people with her quiet and elegant manner. On seeing her, the president of Armenia remarked that she looked Armenian. She was truly a remarkable woman.

I have had a very meaningful life as the spouse of a diplomat, but there was, of course, one major difference in my role: As the male counterpart, I did not have to worry about arrangements of parties, functions and dinners. I attended every function or event, made friends with the locals, diplomats, Indians and professionals. I satisfied my curiosity and used every moment to increase my knowledge about various countries. I was often in the minority, as female spouses were more in number. But this never proved to be an obstacle. In fact, as a spouse, I had the good fortune to attract the affection and love of many in the diplomatic community. Sharing their experiences enriched me in more ways than one.

A Daughter's Perspective

Moscow

SMITA PURUSHOTTAM

I write this as the daughter or Shri S.V. Purushottam, a beloved Indian Foreign Service officer, and on behalf of my late mother, Smt. Susheela Purushottam, who made a huge contribution to my father's career.

My father's first posting was in Moscow in the early 1960s. He became the right-hand man for every Ambassador as he swiftly mastered the Soviet Union's history and contemporary reality. He also picked up perfect Russian. Twenty years later, the examiner declared Papa had done much better than me in the oral Russian exam! From Moscow, my memories consist of nursery (detskiy sad), summer camp, Ded Moroz (an 'atheist' Father Christmas), set against icy blue and silver colours—still my favourite shades—picnics, strawberry–mushroom picking, our embassy basement accommodation, tobogganing down snowy slopes, Napoleon's dacha on the embassy premises and us kids greeting Nikita Khrushchev in an airport line-up

A precious memory stands out. My mother visiting three-year-old me at a Russian summer camp, bringing a slice of tarbuz and making a bracelet of daisies. I now realise why I subconsciously chose tarbuz and its rhyming companion kharbuz for my passwords and first email ID! Another memory is of her describing the terror she felt during the 1962 Cuban missile crisis. Expecting the outbreak of nuclear war, she went to sleep wearing her jewellery, so that future generations would know what they wrought on a peaceful and prosperous world.

Under Khrushchev, the USSR had morphed into a gentler, more open society. Khrushchev was nothing like the caricature the West painted of him. He humanised the USSR after Stalin's diabolical rule and allowed the publication of many dissident works, on which Papa wrote a comprehensive analysis in April 1963. Nobel Laureate Aleksandr Solzhenitsyn credited Khrushchev for permitting the publication of his books *One Day in the Life of Ivan Denisovich* and *The Gulag Archipelago*, revealing the appalling conditions in Stalin's infamous forced labour camps.

Years after my father's passing, I stumbled upon his brilliant insights into Khrushchev's abrupt removal from power, which he attributed to the latter's reforms:

'After Stalin's cruel and senseless rule, Mr Khrushchev created the image of a rational country with a rational leadership .... That image, unfortunately, is broken today ... the development of real democracy in the Soviet Union has suffered a setback. Mr Khrushchev was a man of the people. He, therefore, occasionally displayed a scorn for the omnipotent Party apparatus, which was afraid of him, because he was slowly eroding away the Party's authority and transplanting it into the people. This was heresy and he could not be allowed to proceed.'

Ambassador Tikki Kaul disagreed with Papa, but then the establishment has frequently refused to recognise the obvious.

During my father's two assignments in Moscow, we discovered in the Russians we met an innate decency, warmth, joie de vivre, high literacy levels and a desire to jettison their oppressive past. Hence, we didn't swallow the Western media's exaggerated demonisation of the Russian people, motivated as it was by a geopolitical agenda. Many years later, as Under Secretary (East Europe), I, too, predicted that Mikhail Gorbachev's reforms—perestroika and glasnost—would erode the Communist Party's authority and snowball into a movement for democracy, although the disastrous Western prescriptions for 'shock therapy' under Boris Yeltsin's erratic rule, at a time when Russia desperately needed visionary leadership, encumbered its advance. I, too, was generally pooh-poohed, but at least my boss was attentive to my analysis.

In Papa's next assignment, my recollections centre around quality family time, even though he was a workaholic, as I would later become. We kids witnessed stimulating discussions between my idealistic parents and their colleagues, who still remember the open house my parents hosted. Papa organised picnics, introduced us to contemporary musicals, French pop, the Beatles, Hindi songs and movies, recounted the Dracula story and the plots of *Where Eagles Dare* and *Wait Until Dark* so vividly that the hugely suspenseful movies paled in comparison. He took us on 'home leaves' to Bihar, explained the constellations to us and brightened everyone's lives. But Papa's long work hours were extremely challenging for my mother, as it must be for most IFS spouses, ultimately contributing to his untimely passing at the age of forty-eight. My English tutor, who kindled my creative imagination, wrote a fictional story for me when I was around seven, about a dad who worked twenty-five hours a day and whose dog bit him after failing to recognise him when he returned home.

After several happy years in Delhi, Papa's posting to Washington was abruptly cancelled, because the person he had worked under, then Minister of Commerce Dinesh Singh, had fallen from favour. Papa was sent to Moscow again in 1971 after spending two years in a tiny transit accommodation. My mother was very worried about the impact on my education, as I was now in high school. But soon the Bangladesh crisis erupted in March, and Papa became indispensable to the negotiations that led to the historic Indo-Soviet Treaty in August 1971. He was the only fluent Russian-speaking IFS officer there and enjoyed unprecedented access to and rapport with the Soviet side. A flurry of diplomacy in Moscow under the charismatic Ambassador D.P. Dhar ensued as millions of refugees flooded into India following the atrocities committed by Pakistani troops in East Pakistan, vividly reported by Peter Hazelhurst and Anthony Lewis in the *London Times* and the *International Herald Tribune*, respectively. Although we weren't privy to the official parleys, our Kutuzovsky Prospect flat witnessed many animated discussions between Papa and visiting dignitaries, including D.P. Dhar and the first Bangladeshi Ambassador to Moscow, to which we children listened in rapt attention. It was clear that the conflict was going to draw India in sooner or later. Like many children of our generation, we held our breath while the Soviet Union, under tremendous pressure in the UN Security Council, repeatedly vetoed Western efforts to secure a ceasefire before a decisive outcome was reached. In many ways, we had a ringside seat to the events leading to India's ultimate victory over the aggressors.

Moscow was full of other pleasures. I saw The Bolshoi's *Swan Lake* and *Giselle*, the performance of the legendary dancer Maya Plisetskaya, and Gogol and Dostoyevsky's plays at the Teatr Vakhtangova. Russian literature, with its humanitarian empathy for the oppressed, profound psychological and philosophical depth, biting satire and even humour (Griboyedov, Gogol, Bulgakov, Zoshchenko, even Dostoyevsky in *The Devils*) exerted an enormous pull on me. It was the people's voice, as French was considered the language of the elite. Equally fascinating was its tackling of the existential dilemmas thrown up by Russian and European history—still relevant today. The superfluous man, first embodied in Pushkin's *Eugene Onegin*, described the ennui, redundancy and frustration felt by many talented individuals in a heavily oppressive, unequal society. And Dostoyevsky's character's extraordinarily prescient observation in *Demons*—'Starting from unlimited freedom, I arrive at unlimited despotism'—foreshadowed the totalitarian ideologies of the twentieth century that would underpin Stalinist/Maoist/Nazi terror and their copycat offshoots, contaminating the noble ideals embodied in socialism. Few people know that the ideas Zamyatin presented in *We* foreshadowed Huxley's *Brave New World* and Orwell's *1984*.

Apart from the brilliant writings of Lermontov and other Russian writers, another author who fired my imagination was Mikhail Bulgakov in *The Master & Margarita*, a novel deploying magical realism in hilariously absurd settings, juxtaposed against a searingly realistic description of the crucifixion of a gentle, good man two thousand years ago. The novel introduced the Devil and his cohorts, particularly Behemoth, a walking, talking gigantic black cat, who caroused through Moscow exposing all its warts, hypocrisies, censorship and petty bureaucratism, and punished the collaborators of an increasingly despotic regime. Paradoxically, the Devil was on the side of the Good, and to this day, people have been unable to decipher the full import of this iconoclastic book.

Despite a heavy workload, Papa and Mom organised picnics and get-togethers regularly. My father's colleagues were also fun. When Rajiv and Veena Sikri joined the mission, it became even more lively. My mother, a classical dancer, taught Veena and me how to perform the Alarippu, which we showcased on the embassy stage. Mrs Sikri also tutored me in English.

My strictly vegetarian mom had a tough time in Moscow. The only vegetable available was cabbage, which she had abhorred all her life! Air India flew in vegetables once in a while. Diplomats had an easier time accessing consumer goods in special shops called beriozkas. The unfairness in a 'communist' society was palpable, but standards of living were well above the global average, so we didn't shed hypocritical tears.

Mom was an incredible hostess who could make all sorts of elegant dishes like Baked Alaska and crab soufflé for Papa's diplomatic parties, while Papa ensured the uniqueness of each occasion. In those days, IFS officers' wives were rarely given permission to work abroad. Mom was highly qualified, being the first Bihari woman to earn an M.Sc. in Physics, but she subsumed her aspirations to fulfil the role of a supportive spouse and devoted mother. She held her own in every environment and would not be cowed down when she felt the truth or national interest was at stake. Papa told me during his last visit to Moscow that he had relied on her insights on many issues, as she had an unerring instinct for right and wrong.

My mother was snapped up to teach maths and physics at prestigious high schools in New York, and as a lecturer at Lady Irwin College in Delhi. She also proved her mettle as manager of the Ministry of External Affairs Hostel. She described the various challenges she overcame in her book *Bari Der Kar Di*. She also brought up my son Ashwin, and held our family together after my father's sudden passing. She had been very proud of his idealism and incorruptible character, and she rallied for our sake.

Looking back, it has struck me with the utmost poignancy that we didn't compel our mother to do something for herself. We accepted her sacrifice as an entitlement. My dad also realised this and in the final moments of his life, he called her a goddess. Ambassador Lalit Mansingh, former Foreign Secretary, called her heroic.

I was sent to a Russian summer camp again where I was the centre of attention, made wonderful friends and had unending fun in the beautiful Russian countryside. There was an older boy band that invited me to sing a Beatles song for them, which I bungled. That was the first and last time I joined a rock band. I made a lasting friend there: Tamara Kotikova, a brilliant, beautiful student. We shared many confidences, including on the political scene in the USSR. Those were the days of samizdat and Solzhenitsyn, and I was moved by her trust in me. We had watched an inspiring film on Salvador Allende together, and we both shed tears when he was murdered in a CIA coup.

But the reckoning came when I entered high school. I was fourteen when we were transferred to Moscow. I sank to the bottom of my class because I couldn't understand Russian. I suffered from adolescent angst and being seen as stupid, as I had been a top student and active in sports and extracurricular activities in India. In Moscow, I did well only in maths and chemistry because these were symbol-based subjects. I secretly and frequently bunked class, wandering all day in the beautiful Metro and Gorky Park in -20°C cold. It opened a wound in my psyche that overstayed indefinitely. The girl who went to Moscow was different from the gloomy and underconfident teen who emerged afterwards.

By ninth grade—which was equivalent to India's tenth grade—I was able to deliver a presentation (or rather a eulogy) on Gandhi in Russian. In the discussion that followed, the class felt that the mass movement was deliberately reined in whenever it gained independent momentum, ostensibly in the name of nonviolence, because it suited the elite who didn't want existing property relations to be disturbed. I, too, ended up feeling that a less fettered movement could indeed have swept away the relics of our feudal past and delivered a more honest politics, society and dynamic economy.

Meanwhile, Papa was transferred even though I had just entered my final school year. My mother was furious at this second blow to my education. I was upset too and let Papa know. But after Papa passed away, I found a file which contained plea after plea to the ministry to hold the transfer until I finished my final year of school. I was grief-stricken at how cold-heartedly his appeals had been rejected. Why had the ministry been so callous?

The answer soon came via friendly channels: the orders had come from the top, which explained the ministry's unusual obduracy. The new Ambassador, who was very insecure, had persuaded the prime minister to transfer Papa despite or because of the fine work he had done and his expertise and access to the Soviet hierarchy. My mother used to proudly say that a Politburo member bid Papa farewell in person, which led to much gnashing of teeth from the new Ambassador, who objected strenuously to my dad's meeting with him. My mother also recounted occasions when the Ambassador's British wife insulted Russian officials, which Mom pointed out was detrimental to our bilateral relations. This must have compounded the situation for my father.

Papa was a marvellous and outstanding officer whose contributions were recognised by all. He was kind and generous to a fault, as evidenced by his magnanimous behaviour after the Emergency, which he abhorred. During that time, many, if not all foreign service officers, refused to even acknowledge Mrs Gandhi at official receptions. But my father always went up to her so that she wasn't completely isolated. As he explained to my Mom, who asked why he did it, she had once been our prime minister.

I could only get admission to the BA History course at Delhi University, as my excellent science grades were not accepted for my preferred science course. The transition was more jarring this time. I didn't want to study history, which was not taught in a scientific manner and did not illuminate the progression of historical events.

Another aspect of life in India which impacted me negatively (and still weighs upon me) was the extreme poverty and inequality. The use of English among the elite also struck me as incongruous, as I had seen people taking pride in their mother tongues abroad. In India, we prided ourselves on being cut off from the masses. It was like Russia before the revolution, with the elite speaking French and unconcerned about the poor. Except that in India the poor were too downtrodden to rebel and the leaders too pusillanimous to deliver real change. I felt like a misfit again during my BA years and retreated into a shell.

I turned to social service, but the extreme deprivation I saw knocked the wind out of me. I would return to hot home-cooked meals after leaving emaciated children in Delhi's slums. I quit after the Sanjay Gandhi evictions led to the destruction of the slum. I think I joined the IFS because I couldn't deal with poverty, corruption and exploitation. Later, I learned of the work of idealistic IAS colleagues like Nivedita Haran and my cousin Sanjeeva Kumar, who had successfully improved the lives of millions, and I felt guilty about my abdication. However, I tried to apply the lessons learnt during my China assignment to advise on a better techno-nationalist development model for India and started a trust to promote these ideas. We have made an impact.

Being an astute political observer who was strongly committed to his roots and democratic ideals, Papa had predicted the opposition's clean sweep in the 1977 elections. That historic night we cheered the victory of democracy together as it unfolded before our excited eyes on the news boards of Bahadur Shah Zafar Marg. He later resolved to join politics to find a way to end corruption, which he said was different from that in other countries, as it was rooted in the exploitation and subjugation of the poorest of the poor. I inherited my love for genuine democracy, constitutional propriety and equity from him.

Fortunately, by the time I was pursuing my master's degree I had developed a feel for history under the guidance of my world-renowned professor, Parthasarathy Gupta. I initially used the Marxist framework for historical analysis, but broadened my horizons under his guidance. I also fondly remember Vijay Singh's Twentieth-century European History class in which we had an animated discussion on the Russian Revolution following a thesis I had submitted.

I also published several philosophical articles in *The Statesman* after meeting a charismatic person who stimulated an interest in philosophy and in literature beyond Russian works. I was looking for something out of this world. Not God, though I toyed with that briefly. My antidote for the pervasive feeling of hollowness was to escape into a magical imaginary world populated by ideas and characters from the works of Hesse, Nietzsche, Camus, Sartre, Goethe, Bulgakov, Buddha, Gandhi, Capra, Marx, Monod, etc., so much so that I was called 'Confusius' in university. In my universe, cut off from reality, lasting meaning was always out of reach and, when seemingly attained, turned out to have feet of clay, although traces of stardust continued to linger in my mind.

One thing that always anchored me was my performance in studies, and later my work in the IFS, which I loved passionately. I received 'outstanding' grades in four European MA history courses, taught at Jesus & Mary College and won a fellowship for a PhD at Cornell University. I began to love myself a little again.

It was thanks to Papa that I had earlier appeared for the exam for the IFS. He had returned from a month's absence and found me loitering in my pyjamas on the first day of the main exam and urged me to take a 'one in a million chance'. I cycled down to the Union Public Service Commission centre on Shah Jahan Road, arriving half an hour late, with the examiners looking at me pityingly. Later, I recounted my interview to Papa, who immediately predicted I would get in, but I persisted in thinking I was too dumb to get into Papa's service.

I needed yet another nudge after I got the call, as I still wanted to complete my fully funded Ph.D. at Cornell University. Papa had visited the United States once before and we had listened goggle-eyed while he described the prosperity and abundance there. Yet he used to call daily to persuade me to return to India, and Mom used to call immediately after to persuade me to stay. But Papa won. Thank you, Papa.

I saw Papa twice in Moscow before he passed away. His visits were amazing as he relived his years in Moscow and met friends and colleagues. He cracked jokes, regaled everyone with anecdotes and offered sage advice. He even procured tickets for my beloved *The Master & Margarita* at the Taganka. I had no idea it would be the last time I would see him. He did excuse himself suddenly from a party and alarm bells should have gone off. In New York he continued to work himself to the bone; work always gravitates to the most competent and sincere officers. My mother informed me that he attended conferences for thirty-six hours at a stretch. On the day of his death, a minister landed up and Papa had to cancel an appointment with his quack of a doctor, who had astonishingly failed to recognise serious shortness of breath and extreme fatigue as symptoms of heart trouble. It is difficult to relive those missed opportunities to have prevented his death.

Papa, who had been happy and proud that I had followed his advice of joining the IFS, passed away suddenly. His dreams of resigning from the service to join politics, transforming India and doing away with corruption—dreams he had shared with me in detail—died with him. Hundreds of colleagues in India and abroad paid homage to his memory.

I've worked hard and sincerely during my own stint in the IFS, making original and constructive contributions to my assignments and delivering positive results for the country. Like my colleagues, I have been exposed to extraordinary people and brilliant minds, and have lived in places I would never had had the chance to experience so deeply.

My life has held so much magic because of the sacrifices my parents made, the exposure they gave me and the values they taught me. My parents have been my most precious cornerstone, support and inspiration amidst bewildering change and upheaval. I hope I can give my family a fraction of what my parents gave me.

Marionettes in Disguise

A Conclusion

JAYSHREE MISRA TRIPATHI

For the last thirty years, I have been a part of the 'Indian Foreign Service family'—a small link in a massive chain of strength that spans continents. I deliberately say 'small', as I was a non-working diplomatic spouse and did not directly contribute to the functioning of the mission. I wonder how others view us as we embark on our travels to a distant land. Our children are wrenched from their friends, extended families and comforting environs. Yet, they brave all odds and settle into unfamiliar routines at a new school with dignity, and deserve our commendations. How many of us have sat and cried for hours after the children are off to school and the husband has left for the chancery and we are on our own in a new residence? We have to make it a 'home' for our children while also maintaining a 'representational area' with new local staff.

We enter countries, and as our husbands rise in seniority we often take precedence over the local Indians or people of Indian origin at banquet tables of the host country's president, prime minister or foreign minister. We then plan our tables for local dignitaries, visiting VIPs, diplomatic colleagues and others. We are rated for our hosting of national days. My heart used to beat a hundred times faster as each Independence Day and Republic Day approached, hoping the chosen menu would suit everyone from back home—north, south, east, west, northeast and northwest too—all fellow Indian citizens. They always came first.

Sleepless nights, heart aflutter, wondering if the catered food would be enough for the numberless guests that may or may not arrive for the early morning flag hoisting? On one occasion, we were informed, 'Last year, 350 out of 1,600 invited guests attended.' Since the figures vary from country to country, we ordered an extra hundred plates, just in case. The menu included gravy and dry dishes, vegetarian and non-vegetarian options, cuisine from across the nation, juice galore, mineral water and masala chai. A few years ago, as we sat down after all the guests had left one such function, someone remarked: 'All the spouses should be awarded golden brooches when their husbands retire, fashioned into two samosas and two gulab jamuns, in remembrance of their hard work!' I was not amused. I have yet to skilfully master the art of answering the query 'So what did you do?' without a pause.

Let me pay tribute here to the pioneer women of our service. These women followed their husbands without question, to new posts and missions—even risking their lives at times. One such incident related to us at a meeting involved reminiscences of camping overnight after hours on horseback through difficult terrain, only to discover the next morning that they were pitched on the edge of a ravine! Our trivial complaints about delayed flights pale in comparison. What hardships they endured, what dedication and devotion they displayed. They gave of their lives unstintingly. These are memories I carried with me through difficult postings in distant lands.

A book written by the wife of an overseas colleague used the term 'diplomatic baggage' to describe accompanying spouses, but that is rough on us. Are our lives worthwhile in this fast-paced modern world where women are making their mark across the seas, with salaries that make you gasp for breath? A former college classmate of mine is a retired chief justice of a high court in India, while another heads the overseas division of her company in the USA, yet another is a CEO in the airline industry, another an executive editor, a chief publisher, the principal of a college—the list is endless.

How will I recall the Indian Foreign Service in the years to come? The camaraderie and spirit of mischief when we were younger wives, grumbling about the making of two thousand samosas and gulab jamuns, or our aching feet from standing from six in the morning to nine at night to raise funds annually at various charity bazaars for international women's organisations? Or vowing never to ask for help when we were senior wives, and regretting not being able to muster up the courage to do so, especially given the different times we lived in and the undiplomatic comments we might have been forced to hear? Instead, I paused to relive the fascinating images that captured my spirit when I felt low about not being someone in my own right. How else could I have travelled the world and yet retained the spirit of my country inside me?

Time freezes in the kaleidoscope of past images: of river rafting in Nepal, volunteering at the Paralympics in South Korea, skiing (with not much success!) in Finland, learning to dance the baile in Panama, watching the Chhau dancers from Odisha enthral the audiences in Colombo and observing the fascinating make-up process of the Kathakali troupe in Panama.

I can still feel the sense of unease regarding the airport closure in Antananarivo, just a few days before we were to arrive, and the crisis that ensued for several months thereafter or my disbelief at standing on the shore of the White Nile in Jinja, thinking how calm the water seemed, despite the fiery negotiations on water rights. Or the sadness that lingers, for I still mourn the death of good people we once knew, assassinated for their beliefs.

Then I recall the lighter moments. How, on a wet, dreary afternoon overseas, I watched an 'etiquette expert' on a television programme declare that it is quite all right to eat the following with your fingers: artichoke (pull away the leaf, dip it in sauce, scrape the flesh off the base of the leaf with the top of your teeth and discard the leaf), asparagus, bacon, bread (must be broken, never cut), cookies, corn on the cob, fast foods, hors d'oeuvres, canapés, crudités, sandwiches, small fruits, even berries with stems ... and to leave my napkin neatly to the right of my dinner plate (no refolding) at the end of a meal, after gently dabbing my lips—a far cry from the sorisa machha jhola with rice that can only be eaten, relished rather, with one's fingers at home!

The expert went on to expound that I should never look too tired, too bored, too hungry, too angry, or slouch in my chair; keep social conversations short; avoid talking about topics that evoke opinions or emotions, namely religion, politics, money; and never interrupt anyone's speech or help finish their sentences ... I should never place my purse or evening bag on the table, or retouch my lipstick, or settle my hair, and always remember to send a handwritten thank-you note within twenty-four hours.

On a serious note, customs do differ the world over and it can be non-plussing for a new spouse to encounter the intricacies of a formal Western sit-down dinner with strange vegetables, though such formalities are fast becoming redundant.

What can a new wife do when planning their first representational dinner? What do the terms of attire have to do with the food being served: formal/informal/casual? I have come across 'optional' too, but then, at age forty-five, and after fifteen years in the diplomatic world, nothing fazed me. Why does a person hesitate to call the head of mission's spouse, or for that matter, the other spouses with whom they have yet to form a rapport? If formal dinners were not the norm in a person's home, one cannot blame the little things that may inadvertently be overlooked by the novice.

Of course, a husband-and-wife team effort would be laudable, but diplomats rarely have the time to indulge in the pastime of casting a memorable and different Indian menu. Or maybe they do nowadays? It would be interesting to know. An acquaintance from the West once confessed to agonising for three days over a formal menu for a dinner with local dignitaries.

I often did too.

Then the question of which wines to serve with Indian food (Must we? Moot point.) to complement all the tarkaris, makhanis, Mughlai, handi, kadhai, tawa dishes, etc., and bhajas, chutneys, pulses and pickles. Quite a difficult task if you have always been vegetarian and never had a drink in your life.

The intricacies of the bouquet of each definite French wine or the easy spirit of the young-bodied California? My memories flash unbidden to our very own and very sweet Princess, which was available only in Goa three decades ago. I have tasted other Indian wines since then, the Sula and Grover labels come to mind, but I must commend the Goan sparkling wine, even if it was initially accepted as a 'tolerable table wine' by the French!

Now on to the 'art of conversing'.

Some time ago, while browsing the internet, I came across an interesting article in the *Ottawa Citizen*'s issue of 17 May 1999, written under the pseudonym Vita Urbis: 'Grace is pleased to be back home in Canada for a while. Truth be told, she found the last posting a bit trying, what with the oppressive heat and the flies and the servants you could never really rely on to prepare food properly or hygienically. She had to supervise constantly. Sometimes she actually had to do things herself.

'Grace was ever mindful of Rule Number One in the *Diplomatic Spouses' Guide to Living Abroad*: Be charming and never, ever, utter a single word about anything. Not a word. About anything.

'Grace has been a diplomatic wife extraordinaire for 40 years and has the ability to rise gamely (smile always—at the ready) to whatever demanding occasion his career with External, as she still insists on calling it, has thrown her way.

'Not only can she whip up a gourmet dinner for 12 at an hour's notice (our cooking takes much longer, especially due to the number or variety of dishes we generally tend to serve), is a part of fund-raising galas, the Diplomatic Spouses' Association, and a real sport, as her friends point out and if anyone can measure out her life in sterling silver coffee spoons, she can.'

Familiar thoughts, the world over!

We diplomatic spouses are a global phenomenon, the 'observers', in contrast to our partners, the 'actors' in the world of contemporary diplomacy. Consider this, Professor Petr Skalnik, Czech anthropologist and diplomat, in his article 'Anthropology of Diplomacy: A New Sub-field', talks of a group of anthropologists with experience in diplomacy who were to discuss 'their fascinating experiences in a coveted profession clouded in myth and ritual. How diplomats treat people in their host country, how they relate among themselves as members of a *Corps Diplomatique*, how they work and live together in an embassy and how they cooperate with their home ministry'.

There is not much emphasis on spouses, nor on children, an area of accompanying 'family' that is both sensitive and fraught with complications. These complications can arise from, say, the necessity to work, to continue a career and do research, all the while taking into account the children's schooling and their psychological well-being, as they are continuously uprooted and taken away from friends and relatives. We do not have in-house Counsellors. Teenagers would rather listen to someone else's mother or father. Family Counsellors are necessary to help teenagers cope with the tremendous pressures they face daily in today's complex world. Not everyone can cope. We as a 'family' have grown, and every step has been a learning experience. More and more women are now able to live and work overseas, mainly due to the efforts of the earlier nurturers and leaders. They have shown the way to manage a life of great responsibility. It is this that makes it all worthwhile.

It is the people, all the languages, the religions, even the colours, richness and diversity of our nation that form the very strength of our service. No matter where we are, the Tricolour will always bring tears to the eyes as we listen to the strains of the national anthem or just watch it flutter in the breeze in an alien land.

Still, a question hovers in my mind: Will all the people I have met over three decades reduce me to samosas and gulab jamuns or tandoori chicken with butter naan?

Seriously though, I do hope they will recall my support in their times of need during a family bereavement or a child's christening or a special prayer session. I hope they will have appreciated my helping hand at one of their functions or my speech composed to complement their activity of the year. Will they recall the time I spent visiting hospitals with hampers for the babies born on Independence Day, or my volunteering hours and hours for charity work that often left me drained, both emotionally and physically, for days?

Will my local staff recall my frustration at their careless handling of our crystal (serious matter) or losing my dinner napkins (trivial)? Or my listening to their hopes and aspirations and helping out with some significant contribution before we departed to help them and their children?

Diplomacy has changed drastically in the last decade. New internal rules have come into place too. Many of the gen-next are wary of marrying into the Indian Foreign Service, as they are intent on rising in their own careers. However, accompanying spouses nowadays may work, with permission, in varied professions. They have many opportunities to study, learn new languages, volunteer at schools and charitable organisations, travel into realms once only read about and discover the heritage of new cultures. We have to keep abreast with globalisation and changing trends. We need to modify our styles of representation without losing our identities. It is this very individuality that will temper and enhance whatever new norms we accept. There is no question of aping other nations. We are fortunate to be able to draw from our expansive standard cultural traditions and enrich them in our unique ways. That will be the true hallmark of 'spouse diplomacy' of the future.

Seven years after my late husband retired, in reflection of the decades gone by, I am humbled by the privilege it has been to be a part of India's foreign service. And, I earnestly hope that people will choose to remember me for my undivided attention as I listened to their words. Yes, that would please me!

About the Contributors

Jayshree Misra Tripathi accompanied her husband, Sibabrata Tripathi (IFS 1979), to South Korea, Finland, Panama, Sri Lanka, Madagascar, Uganda and Kenya. She was a consultant and examiner for the International Baccalaureate Organization. After being awarded an 'A' grade in MA English from Delhi University in 1978, she taught where vacancies were available and permissible. Her interest in human rights led her to pursue a PG Diploma in Human Rights Law (2001) through distance education from the National Law School of India University, Bengaluru.

Her books include *The Sorrow of Unanswered Questions*; *Trips and Trials: A Selection of Poems and Songs*; *Children's Verse: Tales from India*; *Uncertain Times* (written during the pandemic); and *What Not Words: Short Stories Set in India and the Diaspora*. Her poems have been published in various international journals, including over the past decade in the *Journal of The Poetry Society (India)*; online: *The Punch Magazine*, *Muse India* and *Madras Courier*; and articles in *The Huffington Post* and News18. As the eldest of five daughters, Jayshree includes her maiden surname in her writing.

Ajay Shankar (IAS 1973) is married to Meera Shankar (IFS 1973). Meera was the first woman Ambassador to Germany and then the first woman professional to be the Ambassador to the USA, the first one being Prime Minister Nehru's sister. Ajay retired as Secretary in the Department of Industrial Policy and Promotion (DIPP) in the Government of India. He played a key role in putting together the stimulus packages that facilitated the speedy recovery of the Indian economy after it was hit by the 2008 global financial crisis, processing the enactment of the Electricity Act, 2003, sanctioning of the Rural Electrification Programme, which paved the way for the completion of household electrification, and designing the National Solar Mission.

He writes opinion pieces and papers on energy and economic policy and is a Distinguished Fellow at The Energy and Resources Institute (TERI) and the Institute for Studies in Industrial Development (ISID). He is also associated with several NGOs.

Anita Sapra is married to a career diplomat and is the mother of three children and has four super grandchildren. She has had the opportunity of living in Australia, Bhutan, Saudi Arabia, Spain, South Korea, Kuwait, North Korea, the United Kingdom, the Caribbean islands of Trinidad and Tobago, Grenada, the Commonwealth of Dominica and Montserrat. An educator by profession, she has taught both adults and school children at all levels in British and American systems of education. The focus of her teaching has been in the field of information and technology along with English as a second language. Her longest teaching period was at the American Embassy School in New Delhi.

Anuradha Muthukumar was born in India but brought up in countries as diverse as the USA and Nepal. She completed her education in India, becoming an alumna of Scindia Kanya Vidyalaya, Gwalior, and then Jawaharlal Nehru University, Delhi. At JNU, she joined a five-year integrated language programme in Spanish but switched after a year to Japanese when the School of Languages established a master's programme. Anuradha speaks five foreign languages and three Indian languages. A four-year gap and limited opportunities for Japanese-speaking professionals led to a career in garment exports, which was a burgeoning industry at the time, with manufacturing units coming up all over India. Many moons later, returning to India after another bout of diplomatic life, an opportunity arose that took her back to languages, where she began training young adults, senior corporate managers/CEOs, housewives, etc., in spoken English and soft skills. She is married to B.R. Muthukumar.

Ashok Pandey is a gold medallist in BA and MA from Bihar University. He acquired a PhD in public administration. Born in Bihar, he taught at Ranchi University for a couple of years and joined the IAS in 1965. Initially in the Assam/Meghalaya cadre, he served in Nagaon, Karimganj and Shillong. Ashok was involved in the refugee relief work in Meghalaya after the 1971 India–Pakistan War. He served in Delhi in various capacities in the ministries of defence, commerce and labour. He did a one-year course in Manchester, UK, and a three-month management course in Henley, UK. In 1984, his cadre was changed to Bihar, where he served as food commissioner and later as executive director of the Food Corporation of India and subsequently as member of the electricity board and energy commissioner in Patna.

In 1993, he married Reena Poovaiah, who was in the foreign service. From 1993 until his retirement, he was on deputation to the Lok Sabha Secretariat in the Speaker's Office. During this period, he visited many countries as part of parliamentary delegations led by the Lok Sabha Speaker. He was with Reena in her postings to London, Istanbul, Armenia and Georgia. In 2016, his book *From Inside the Steel Frame: The Memoirs of an Administrator* was published by Palimpsest Publishing House. *Local Level Planning and Rural Development: An Analytical Study* (1990) was based on his research for his PhD degree. His essays and poems in Hindi have been published in reputed journals like *Aaj Kal*.

Asiya Hamid Rao graduated with a first division in English literature from Aligarh Muslim University. She completed her higher studies after marriage, with a master's from Miranda House, Delhi University, and a PhD from Jamia Millia Islamia, Delhi. Although a student of English literature, a special place in her heart forever remained reserved for Urdu poetry. She was actively involved in co-curricular activities in school and college, and won several awards for debate, elocution and drama.

From the late 1980s to the late 1990s, Asiya regularly contributed middles and human-interest stories to national dailies such as *The Pioneer*, *Hindustan Times*, *The Times of India* and others.

A teacher by profession, Asiya has taught in schools in Delhi, Vienna, Geneva and at a private university in Dhaka. In 2006, while teaching at Sanskriti School, New Delhi, Asiya was the recipient of several awards at 'Unsung Heroes, No Longer', a competition for school teachers organised by Mumbai's Rustom Irani Foundation. These included awards for 'Student-Teacher Interaction', the 'Turncoat' round and 'Best Out of Waste'. She won first place in the zonal round and represented North India zone in the finals held in Mumbai.

Asiya is married to Hamid Ali Rao (IFS 1981) and accompanied him to postings in Vienna, Geneva, Dhaka, Riyadh and The Hague.

Hema Devare is a gold medallist from Nagpur University. A freelance writer, Hema has contributed to leading newspapers. She is the author of several books, including her latest Marathi novel *Rajneetichya Hindolyavar* (a work of fiction on diplomacy), and *Ganga to Mekong: A Cultural Voyage through Textiles*. Her first book published in 1993, *Vishwa Videsh Seveche* (in Marathi), was about life in the foreign service. Hema wrote two Hindi plays, *Bahu Pardeski* and *Anokha Rishta*, which were staged in Frankfurt and Indonesia. She also wrote dance dramas, *Bali Yatra* and *Swapna Sakaram*, that were staged in Southeast Asia on behalf of the Indian Council for Cultural Relations. She produced a book, *Saree Sutra*, about the similarities between Indian and Indonesian textiles and a documentary film, *Threads That Bind*, on cultural ties between the two countries. Married to Sudhir Devare (IFS 1964), Hema accompanied him to the Soviet Union, the USA, Sikkim, Switzerland, Burma, South Korea, Germany, Ukraine and Indonesia.

Kusum Budhwar honed her talent as a writer when she bought her first computer in 1995 in Canada, where her husband was then posted as India's High Commissioner. Learning keyboard skills gave birth to her first book, *Romance of the Mango: The Complete Book of the King of Fruits* (Penguin, 2002), followed by a second, *Where God's Dwell: Folktales of India* (Penguin, 2007). She has written articles covering travel, religion, folklore and cookery, and has been published in various magazines and books. Her master's degree in History of Fine Arts was an asset that brought greater appreciation of the cultures of other nations. As a trained teacher, she taught at the Convent of Jesus & Mary (CJM) Waverley, Mussoorie; Naval Public School, Delhi; and Kendriya Vidyalaya, Moscow. Her hobbies include knitting, decorative painting on wood and photography. She is married to Prem Budhwar (IFS 1962). Their postings included the erstwhile Soviet Union, Hong Kong, Vietnam, Germany, Ethiopia, Brazil and Canada. They have two sons and three grandchildren. After retirement, since 1997, their winters are spent in Delhi and summers in Mukteshwar, Uttarakhand.

Kusum Tayal retired from a public-sector bank in 2021 and is the wife of Skand Ranjan Tayal (IFS 1976). She has a keen interest in travel, reading (both fiction and non-fiction) and sports, especially swimming and table tennis. She enjoys playing the piano and watching tennis. She studied Economics at Jesus and Mary College, Delhi, and was captain of the college volleyball team and has won college-level chess tournaments. She has accompanied her husband to Johannesburg and Houston, where he was the Consul General, and to Tashkent and Seoul, where he was the Ambassador. At present, she serves in an advisory capacity on the board of Amar Jyoti Charitable Trust, a school that provides inclusive education for children of different abilities alongside regular children.

Margreta Kumar, née Suting, was born in Shillong, Meghalaya, 'the Abode of the Clouds'. She did her schooling and college in Shillong and went on to do her M.Sc. in Food Technology at the prestigious Central Food Technological Research Institute in Mysore, Karnataka. She worked as a professor at St. Mary's College, teaching biochemistry, microbiology, food and nutrition.

Margreta is married to Ajit Kumar (IFS 1979), who retired in 2017 as the Permanent Representative of India to the United Nations in Geneva. They have two children who are now settled in the USA.

Margreta speaks Spanish fluently and a smattering of French and German. Having passed her Grade 8 piano exam from the prestigious Trinity College London, she plays the piano occasionally. She has now turned entrepreneur and runs her heritage home in Shillong as an Airbnb. Her goal is to be bold, creative and forward thinking. She also runs a fortnightly formal sit-down dinner called 'The Ambassador's Table', where she showcases to her guests a themed cuisine from a particular country she has visited, blending in a bit of history and culture.

Her other passions include spending time in nature, enjoying music, dancing, Pilates, fabric painting and Ikebana. She also enjoys writing short stories and poems and is an avid lover of pets, especially dogs.

Her aim is to inspire and be inspired.

Preeti Singh began her career as a Lecturer at Indraprastha College for Women, Delhi (1972), and completed her PhD programme from The George Washington University (1987). After early retirement from Indraprastha College as a Reader (1996), she worked at Oxford University Press, New Delhi. Preeti has led a peripatetic life, being married to a diplomat, Ambassdor Swashpawan Singh (IFS 1974). Her experiences in different parts of the world have been the inspiration behind her creative writing. Her first novel, *Circles of Silence* (2002), is set in Cairo and New Delhi. She is currently working on her next book, titled *The Bird Sanctuary*, which is about the Indian immigrant experience in Texas, USA. Preeti also works as a freelance professional editor for various publications and institutions, including for the Association for Indian Diplomats and the Institute for Defence Studies and Analyses, among others.

Reshmi Ray Dasgupta is a journalist. Her father, Ambassador A.K. Ray, was born and raised in East Bengal and was one of the first to enter the IFS via examination in 1950. Her mother, the daughter of a senior civil servant, was born in Prayagraj and grew up all over north India, including Delhi. As an IFS child, Reshmi imbibed not only her parents' innate curiosity about and interest in different cultures and people but also their fierce love for India and everything Indian, which is reflected in her career as a journalist with *The Economic Times*. She remains a lifelong fan of IFS spouses.

Sharmila Kantha is a consultant with the Confederation of Indian Industry (CII) and has been associated with Indian industry since 2004, working extensively on macroeconomic and industrial policy, manufacturing and competitiveness, and India's international economic engagement. She is the author of several books on Indian business. She contributes articles and columns on economic issues to the media and curates and edits in-house books for CII. She has also published five fiction books for adults and children. Previously, she worked as an officer in a public-sector bank.

Sharmila is the wife of Ashok K. Kantha (IFS 1977). She has been part of the diplomatic community in Beijing, Washington, DC, Kathmandu, Hong Kong, Kuala Lumpur, Colombo and Beijing. Her husband served as Consul General in Hong Kong, High Commissioner in Malaysia and Sri Lanka, Secretary (East) in the Ministry of External Affairs and Ambassador in China.

Shreedevi Nair Pal has had a varied career as a school teacher, banker, copy editor, copy writer and independent researcher on Indian art. She completed her undergraduate and master's degree in English Literature at Presidency College, Calcutta. In 1998, she earned a master's degree in Art History from Delhi's National Museum Institute of the History of

Art, Conservation and Museology, followed by a PhD from the same institute.

Along with her husband, Satyabrata Pal (IFS 1972), she has lived in Baghdad, Jeddah, New York, Botswana, London, South Africa and Pakistan. She buttresses housewifery with her various other interests. She collects and researches colonial-period painting and metalware; old lamps, textiles and maps of India; and books on art history, history, religion, feminism, mother goddess cults and cooking. She also chases words from English, Malayalam, Bengali and Hindi to their lair to discover their origins. And she still bakes her own bread.

Shrimi Sinha did her schooling at various places in India and England. She graduated with a degree in commerce and got married soon after. She accompanied her husband, Dilip Sinha (IFS 1978), on his postings abroad. After becoming a mother of two at a young age, she focused on her role as a mother and hostess. Once in India, when her sons went to school, she pursued a B. Ed. and found her much-loved vocation as a nursery school teacher. She also taught in the nursery sections of the international schools of Geneva and Dhaka. Additionally, she served as the honorary president of the Women's International Club of Athens.

She loves travelling, reading, practising yoga and hanging out with friends. Her husband retired as Ambassador/Permanent Representative to the United Nations in Geneva. She is blessed with two lovely granddaughters.

Smita Purushottam is the daughter of S.V. Purushottam, who joined the IFS in 1959 and passed away in 1983. She accompanied her father on his assignments to Moscow, Geneva and Moscow. She joined the IFS in 1980 and served in India's missions in Berne, Caracas, Berlin, London, Beijing, Brussels and Moscow, as well as on the Russian, South Asian Association for Regional Cooperation, Bhutan and Integrated Defence Staff desks in the Ministry of External Affairs/Ministry of Defence. She took sabbaticals at Harvard, the Institute for Defence Studies and Analyses and other institutions, and has published work on economic and technological reforms. After retirement, she founded the Science, Indigenous Technology & Advanced Research Accelerator.